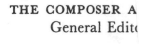

THE COMPOSER A
General Edit

D0663085

Brit

General editor's preface

A series of books needs a personality of its own. As its title suggests *The Composer as Contemporary* offers a distinctly individual approach to a composer and his music, whether he be a Beethoven, a Schubert, a Britten or a Janáček. Each book opens with a detailed account of the original performance of a major work, describing how it was received by its first audience and some of the influences that brought about its composition. Subsequent chapters deal with, in addition to the composer's biography, such topics as the contemporary world to which he responded, the musical forms he chose to work in, his reputation then and now. Above all it is the purpose of the books to establish the composer in the context of his lifetime and consider his music as the expression of its age.

John Lade

Forthcoming titles in the series:

Beethoven   Robert Philip
Janáček   Patrick Lambert
Purcell   Eric Van Tassell
Schubert   Peter Gammond

Britten

CHRISTOPHER HEADINGTON

HM

HOLMES & MEIER
Publishers, Inc.
New York

*For Gerald, Jane, Mark, Nicholas, Jeremy
and Emma Bale with love*

First published in the United States of America 1982 by
Holmes & Meier Publishers, Inc.
30 Irving Place, New York, N.Y. 10003

First published in the United Kingdom 1981 by Eyre Methuen Ltd.

Library of Congress Cataloging in Publication Data

Headington, Christopher.
  Britten.

  (The Composer as contemporary)
  Bibliography: p.
  Includes index.
  1. Britten, Benjamin, 1913-1976. 2. Composers—
England—Biography. I. Title. II. Series: Composer
as contemporary.
ML410.B853H4 1982   780'.92'4 [B]   82-1027
ISBN 0-8419-0802-8   AACR2
ISBN 0-8419-0803-6 (pbk.)

Printed in the United States of America

Contents

List of illustrations   vi
Acknowledgements   vii
Preface by Sir Lennox Berkeley   xi
 1 The Wells, 7 June 1945   1
 2 A boy and his background (1913–33)   16
 3 Young professionalism: Auden and Pears (1934–39)   29
 4 America (1939–41)   45
 5 In wartime England (1942–45)   59
 6 From Glyndebourne to East Anglia (1946–48)   72
 7 Aldeburgh and London (1949–53)   91
 8 West meets east (1954–63)   109
 9 With Aschenbach in Venice (1964–76)   126
10 A time there was ... (1977–81)   146
Selected bibliography   160
Index   162

List of illustrations

Illustrations follow page 86

Working on *Peter Grimes* *(Boosey & Hawkes)*

Peter Pears as Peter Grimes *(Angus McBean)*

Kenneth Green's design for Borough High Street *(Boosey & Hawkes)*

The Britten family *(Britten Estate)*

Benjamin with Mr and Mrs Frank Bridge *(Britten Estate)*

Britten with W.H. Auden *(Auden Estate)*

Pears and Britten painted by Kenneth Green *(National Portrait Gallery)*

A poster for *Paul Bunyan* *(New York Public Library)*

Britten and Pears in Aldeburgh *(Britten Estate)*

The Maltings at Snape *(John Donat)*

Noye's Fludde in rehearsal *(Kurt Hutton)*

Britten with Pears, André Previn and Elisabeth Söderström *(Nigel Luckhurst)*

Britten watching the filming of *Owen Wingrave* *(BBC Photograph)*

Britten in Venice, 1975 *(Britten Estate)*

Acknowledgements

I could not have written this book without the generous help of a number of people who talked to me about Benjamin Britten, some briefly and others at considerable length. These include The Very Revd Dr Walter Hussey, Lord and Lady Redcliffe-Maud, Mrs Beth Welford and Sir Lennox Berkeley – to whom I am eternally grateful for introducing me to Britten over thirty years ago. Lord and Lady Maud and Mr Richard Pantcheff have most kindly made available to me their Britten correspondence. My friend Mr Simon Nowell-Smith helped me over various matters concerning Peter Burra and William Plomer. But pride of place here must go to Sir Peter Pears, who gave me some hours of his time and was unfailingly patient and helpful over innumerable biographical matters. *Amor, pietà, mercè; cose si rare* ...

My friend Dr Donald Mitchell, the composer's publisher and friend and also the Literary Executor of the Britten Estate, has also been generous with his time and with the fruits of his own devoted yet passionately truthful Britten scholarship. He allowed me to see the text, at that time not yet published, of his 1979 T. S. Eliot Memorial Lectures, *Britten and Auden in the Thirties: The Year 1936*; and I have also drawn upon his *Times Literary Supplement* article on the same subject (15 February 1980).

The three BBC radio programmes called *Britten: The Early Years*, broadcast in the spring of 1980 and compiled by Dr Mitchell, have yielded much material. So indeed have an earlier radio programme, *Birth of an Opera: Peter Grimes*, by Michael Rose and Hallam Tennyson, broadcast on 28 September 1976, and, notably, Tony Palmer's documentary biography of the composer, *A time there was* ..., shown on London Weekend Television on Easter Sunday 1980. I am grateful for permission to reproduce this copyright material, as also material from a number of books: *Benjamin Britten: A commentary on his works from a group of specialists* (ed. Donald Mitchell and Hans Keller); *British Composers in Interview* (Murray Schafer); *Ausflug Ost* (Ludwig Prince of Hesse and the Rhine, privately printed); *Aldeburgh Anthology* (ed. Ronald Blythe); *Tribute to Benjamin Britten on his Fiftieth Birthday* (ed. Anthony Gishford); *Benjamin Britten: His Life and Operas* (Eric Walter White); *Britten* (Imogen Holst), 3rd edition; *On Receiving the First Aspen Award* (Benjamin Britten); *Armenian Holiday* (Peter Pears, privately printed); *The Music of Benjamin Britten* (Peter Evans); *The Operas of Benjamin Britten* (ed. David Herbert) and the *Autobiography* of William Plomer. I am indebted to the Executors of the Britten Estate for permission to quote from unpublished Britten letters and extracts (already published) from his diaries. The poem on page 153 is reproduced by permission of W. H. Auden's publishers, Faber & Faber Ltd. The brief quotations from Britten's music are included by permission of his publishers Boosey & Hawkes and Faber Music Ltd. I express my thanks also to Rosamund Strode, Britten's assistant from 1964, and Fred Ferry at the Britten-Pears Library in Aldeburgh and to Sir Peter Pears's secretary, Mrs Peggy Henley.

I am particularly grateful to my old friend and colleague John Lade who, as editor of *The Composer as Contemporary* series, invited me to write this book. Without him, evidently, the book would not have been written, and furthermore during the writing of it his support and advice have been invaluable. My thanks also to Bob Woodings, the editorial director at Eyre Methuen responsible for the project, for tactfully and skilfully steering it towards completion.

Christopher Headington
Beckley, October 1980

Preface

It is now many years since the day when I sat in my room at the Royal Academy of Music awaiting my first pupil. I was feeling depressed and inadequate. How was I who found (and still find) composition so difficult going to teach anyone else how to set about it? These gloomy thoughts were somewhat dispelled when a young man of pleasant appearance entered. I looked at my list of pupils. His name was Christopher Headington. Thus began a friendship that has lasted for over thirty years.

In the course of our meetings we made a special study of the music of Benjamin Britten. We shared a love of it and found that it lent itself very well to analysis. The composer's truly astonishing musical ability, showing a grasp of form, style and meaningful sound, was a fascinating study. I had already got to know his music well and was convinced that he had a great future. Many of the critics of his early music were less impressed, and I was often told that he was merely another clever young man whose music altogether lacked substance and would not pass the test of time. I remained of the opposite opinion and am proud today to have been one of his very first admirers.

This book tells the story of Britten's life, not by separating the life from the music, but by treating the two things concurrently. I feel that the author was right in doing so as Britten's life was very much bound up with his work, indeed one could say that his life was his work. He had a strong sense of his vocation as a composer and would allow nothing to interfere with it. In this book Mr Headington examines closely and with rare perception all the principal works and accords at least a mention to the smaller ones. Especially interesting is his description of how the operas came into being – generally after long discussions with friends and advisers, the choice of a librettist being one of the most important things discussed. Here the names of Eric Crozier and Myfanwy Piper stand out as having achieved brilliant success with *Albert Herring* and *The Turn of the Screw* respectively. In the case of *A Midsummer Night's Dream*, Britten himself and Peter Pears devised the libretto very successfully. Here of course it was a question of how much one could leave out without damaging the play; the same problem that had faced Boito in adapting *Othello* for Verdi. Neither opera starts at the beginning of the play; Boito in fact leaves out the whole of Shakespeare's first act. In neither case does the play seem to suffer – indeed a musical masterpiece results in both.

Christopher Headington writes very movingly about Britten's death and the two years leading up to it. When it became clear that he had little time to live, Britten faced the situation with courage and calm. After a period of being too ill to write he got better for a time and was able to work again. These last works are of great originality and beauty.

This is a book that all who loved and appreciated this great musician should read.

Lennox Berkeley
February 1981

1

The Wells,
7 June 1945

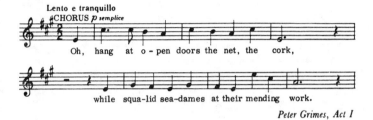

Lento e tranquillo

CHORUS *p semplice*

Oh, hang at o - pen doors the net, the cork,

while squa-lid sea-dames at their mending work.

Peter Grimes, Act I

It was one month after Germany's surrender and the end of the
European war, and the Sadler's Wells Opera Company were
giving the first performance of Benjamin Britten's opera *Peter
Grimes*. With this opera by a young native composer – Britten was
thirty-one – they were taking a risk, for the occasion was an
important one: the reopening of their London theatre after
nearly five years. Right up to the moment when the curtain rose
at a quarter to seven, there were doubts as to the wisdom of
choosing *Peter Grimes* rather than a popular repertory opera for
the reopening; for failure, or even a mere *succès d'estime*, would
have cast a serious shadow over the company's future. Fortunately *Peter Grimes* was a triumph. In the words of Britten's first
biographer, Eric Walter White, 'all who were present realised
that *Peter Grimes*, as well as being a masterpiece of its kind,
marked the beginning of an operatic career of great promise and
perhaps also the dawn of a new period when English opera
would flourish in its own right'.

The inception of *Peter Grimes* went back four years, to the
summer of 1941. Britten, together with the singer Peter Pears,
was at that time living in America, and the two men spent part
of that summer in California as the guests of the pianists Ethel

Bartlett and her husband Rae Robertson. One day they came across a copy of the BBC publication *The Listener*, dated 29 May 1941, containing a reprint of a broadcast talk by E. M. Forster on the Suffolk poet George Crabbe. This at once caught Britten's imagination. For Crabbe (1754–1832) was born at Aldeburgh, not far from Britten's own birthplace Lowestoft, and his poem 'The Borough', published in 1810, describes the life and character of that coastal town of East Anglia. Five years later, Britten was to write: 'I did not know any of the poems of Crabbe at that time, but reading about him gave me such a feeling of nostalgia for Suffolk, where I had always lived, that I searched for a copy of his works, and made a beginning with "The Borough".'

Aldeburgh is neither a romantic nor an especially picturesque town. It was once described (by the author M. R. James in his ghost story 'A Warning to the Curious') as having

> a long sea-front and a street: behind that a spacious church of flint, with a broad, solid western tower and a peal of six bells. How well I remember their sound ... a belt of old firs, wind-beaten, thick at the top, with the slope that old seaside trees have; seen on the skyline from the train they would tell you in an instant, if you did not know it, that you were approaching a windy coast.

That church, with its bells – which were to feature memorably in Act II of *Peter Grimes* – belongs also to George Crabbe's Aldeburgh. Crabbe was brought up in the town, where his father was a collector of salt-duties; he became an apprentice to a doctor, met his future wife Sarah and finally became curate in 1781. He stayed in Aldeburgh for some thirty years.

E. M. Forster characterised Crabbe: 'though a clergyman, he is by no means an "old dear" ... he disapproved, he reproved. Disapproval ... gives his work a curious flavour, subtle yet tart.' As for the setting of 'The Borough', Aldeburgh itself earned from Forster the same wry admiration that he accorded the poet:

> A bleak little place; not beautiful ... It huddles round a flint-towered church and sprawls down to the North Sea – and what a wallop the sea makes as it pounds at the shingle! Near

by is a quay, at the side of an estuary, and here the scenery becomes melancholy and flat; expanses of mud, saltish commons, the marsh-birds crying. Crabbe heard that sound and saw that melancholy, and they got into his verse.

It was this article in *The Listener* that crystallised Britten's growing feeling of rootlessness in America and, as he said, 'evoked a longing for the realities of that grim and exciting seacoast around Aldeburgh'. He and Peter Pears, already home-sick, finally decided to return to England as soon as possible. And in the meantime, Pears had discovered a copy of Crabbe's *Life and Poetical Works* in a secondhand bookshop in San Diego. He and Britten read through 'The Borough' and found the poem both exciting and moving. In Letter XXII of the twenty-four 'Letters' that make up the whole poem Crabbe narrated the sombre story of the lonely fisherman Peter Grimes.

It was probably Peter Pears who first suggested that the story of Grimes might be made into an opera; but as he himself has said, his ideas and Britten's were so close that it is impossible to be sure at this distance of time. 'Either of us might have said it, and together we'd have picked it up.' The two men started work, sketching out various dramatic sections. Initially, of course, it was the setting of Crabbe's poem that attracted Britten, the Suffolk coastal scenes which he knew so well from his child-hood, and the poet's evocation of small-town life. But fortunately Peter Grimes himself provided a highly dramatic story, a *sine qua non* for opera. At the same time he created a problem; for arguably an opera would need a hero, and Crabbe's Grimes was not far from villainous: he was based upon a real Aldeburgh fisherman whose boy apprentices disappeared suspiciously until the townspeople intervened and threatened him with a murder charge. In the poem he has no less than three dead apprentices: this, the poet himself tells us, was a character 'untouched by pity, unstung by remorse, and uncorrected by shame'.

It was clear to Britten and Pears that their operatic Peter Grimes had to be different if he was to win an audience's sym-pathy. And there was a second, more subtle reason. Britten's view of human nature was essentially compassionate; Crabbe's acid disapproval was not in him. His Grimes was to become a

Byronic figure at odds with society: a person self-willed and proud, yet sensitive, who loves and suffers, caring for his friend Ellen Orford and even for his young apprentice John – though he is to harm the one psychologically and to ill-treat the other physically. Yet a third reason lay in what Pears has called 'the relationship between the single man and society'. Britten already knew the 'outsider' feeling of an artist addressing an unresponsive public, and also that associated with his close friendship with Peter Pears; he foresaw the problems that would meet him as a pacifist in wartime England. As he himself put it:

> A central feeling for us was that of the individual against the crowd, with ironic overtones for our own situation. As conscientious objectors we were out of it. We couldn't say we suffered physically, but naturally we experienced tremendous tension. I think it was partly this feeling which led us to make Grimes a character of vision and conflict, the tortured idealist he is, rather than the villain he was in Crabbe.

The ideas for *Peter Grimes* were there; and they grew. Yet there was a long way to go before the eventual realisation of a musical score, and still further before its acceptance and production by an opera company. True, Britten's experience as a song-writer went back to his childhood; however, his one previous operatic venture, *Paul Bunyan*, had failed when it was performed in 1941 in New York. In the meantime, he was still in America, waiting on the East Coast to obtain a sea passage home to England. But the enforced delay of some months proved fortunate as far as the projected opera was concerned. In January 1942 he attended a performance of his *Sinfonia da Requiem* under Serge Koussevitzky in Boston.

> He asked why I had not written an opera. I explained that the construction of a scenario, discussions with a librettist, planning the musical architecture, composing preliminary sketches, and writing nearly a thousand pages of orchestral score, demanded a freedom from other work which was an economic impossibility for most young composers. Koussevitzky was interested in my project for an opera based on Crabbe, although I did not expect to have the opportunity of

writing it for several years. Some weeks later we met again, when he told me that he had arranged for the commissioning of the opera, which was to be dedicated to the memory of his wife, who had recently died.

Two months later, Britten and Pears sailed for England. The ship was a small Swedish cargo boat with some passenger accommodation, the *Axel Johnson*: they boarded at New York, but the ship made its way up the coast (with various stops) to Halifax, Nova Scotia, before the actual Atlantic crossing, so that the voyage took a full month. During this time Britten composed two vocal pieces, the *Hymn to St Cecilia* and *A Ceremony of Carols*. But he found time to do further work on the *Peter Grimes* synopsis. Pears recalls:

> What I did discover in that old Crabbe volume a few years ago were the sketches which Ben and I (in my handwriting in fact) made of the first shape, the first kind of scenario, of *Grimes*, on fading paper with a print of the ship at the top. Thereafter of course, I really came to the conclusion, much as I should like to have written the libretto, that I simply wasn't capable. And so we asked Montagu instead.

Pears is referring to Montagu Slater. He was a poet and novelist with whom Britten had worked on two puppet films in 1938. Now, in wartime England, he worked in the Films Unit of the Ministry of Information but managed to carry on with his own writing by getting up at five in the morning. He seemed to Britten the best available choice as a librettist; and so he was approached, and he accepted. The future producer of *Peter Grimes*, Eric Crozier, recalled him in a BBC programme of 1976:

> A small, taciturn, pipe-smoking, very reserved person, who I think had a deep vein of passion, of sympathy for the working classes, for the underdog in any situation, and who certainly was for that reason a good choice as librettist for *Peter Grimes*. But he wasn't the easiest person in the world to deal with, in relation to the text that he'd drafted. Britten and I would talk, we'd take, say, a particular scene, and discuss the characterisation for that scene, the actual text that we had before us, and we would make suggestions for making it clearer,

more expressive. And Monty would sit smoking his pipe opposite us – and when we had finished our persuasive best, he would sit silent.

Peter Pears puts it rather more bluntly: 'It was hard work, one way and another, because Montagu was not very prolific – he was a slow writer, and found it difficult to produce what Ben wanted.'

Though the writing of the *Peter Grimes* text was a slow process, it was ready as a complete draft by the end of 1943. In the meantime Britten was writing other vocal pieces and gaining valuable experience. Finally, in January 1944, he settled down to sustained work on *Grimes*, interrupted only by the composition of two choral miniatures for a BBC programme, and the vocal score of the opera was ready in February 1945.

Despite his extensive experience with vocal and dramatic music – for besides the operetta *Paul Bunyan* he had contributed music to over thirty plays and films – Britten was still a novice in entering the field of full-length English opera. He told the producer Eric Crozier that he missed having a musical tradition in which to work. He had set plenty of English texts, French and Italian too, but these were not of the same dramatic kind. For opera, he had to find a musical language that would have vitality in recitative (which is otherwise stiff and dull) but could also flower into real tunes. This idea of 'tunes' was important. He was not much attracted by the Wagnerian technique of 'permanent melody', preferring the practice of Mozart, Verdi or Smetana, who wrote what he called 'separate numbers that crystallise and hold the emotion of a dramatic situation at chosen moments'. And he did eventually find the musical language he was looking for. The recitatives in *Grimes*, for example the exchanges at the beginning of the pub scene in Act I, do as he hoped they would 'transform the natural intonations and rhythms of everyday speech into memorable musical phrases'. As for melody, '*Peter Grimes* has got plenty of tunes'; Peter Pears though added that 'maybe to the totally unsophisticated they sound strange at first.'

After his return with Britten to England, Peter Pears had joined the Sadler's Wells Opera Company in 1943, and he was soon singing leading roles in such operas as *Così fan tutte* and *The Magic Flute*, *La Traviata* and *Rigoletto*, *La Bohème* and *The Bartered Bride*. During these wartime years the company was on a kind of permanent tour, excluded from its London theatre which had been converted into a rest centre. Because of Pears's involvement, Britten attended some of the rehearsals and performances; consequently the company got to know him, while he also came to appreciate the company's qualities. In February 1944, just after starting to compose *Peter Grimes*, Britten said in an interview: 'I am passionately interested in seeing a successful permanent national opera in existence – successful both artistically and materially. And it must be vital and contemporary, too, and depend less on imported "stars" than on a first-rate, young and fresh, permanent company. Sadler's Wells have made a good beginning.'

It was shortly after this that Britten travelled to Liverpool, where the Sadler's Wells Company was on tour, and played through the Prologue and Act I of *Peter Grimes* to the artistic director Joan Cross and some of her colleagues – the administrator Tyrone Guthrie, the conductor Lawrance Collingwood and the young producer Eric Crozier. 'It made the most terrific impression,' Joan Cross later recalled. 'I think I wasn't alone in my immediate reaction, that this was the piece to reopen Sadler's Wells when the finish of the war came.' She was supported by Collingwood and Guthrie in deciding to mount the new production, for which some public funds were made available by the Council for the Encouragement of Music and the Arts (CEMA). As for the date of the *Grimes* première, this depended clearly upon the ending of hostilities in Europe, but it was felt that this could not be far off. As it turned out, Britten finished the opera at exactly the right moment: he put the last touches to the orchestral score a few weeks before Germany surrendered.

Britten, who was always stimulated by the practical, wrote later that 'the qualities of the Opera Company considerably influenced both the shape and the characterisation of the opera'. What he called the 'musical architecture' was, however, a more personal matter, and this was something that belonged to an early stage in planning. This is how Eric Crozier put it:

My impression was that he worked from forms towards detail in all the time that I worked with him. It seemed to me that he thought first in terms of shapes, of balancing sections, fast sections against slow sections, rather like an architect planning a building. In fact there was an occasion when I discovered shortly before the production of *Peter Grimes* that he hadn't allowed enough time in one of the interludes for the scene change to take place. That was in the first act, between the scene of the beach and the scene of the pub, the storm interlude. Now the stage at Sadler's Wells was extremely shallow, and there was very little room for getting scenery off at the side. And so after thinking about it seriously, I went to Ben and told him I was extremely sorry, but we needed one and a half minutes more music so that the scene change could be done with absolute safety. It was fast music at that. And Ben resisted for a time. But at last he looked at me rather sourly and said: 'You're like someone who comes along to an architect when he has just finished building a cathedral and gives him a huge block of stone and says, "You simply must find room for this".'

By the time rehearsals for *Peter Grimes* began – in a Methodist hall in Sheffield, a Birmingham gymnasium or the Wolverhampton Civic Hall, all between giving eight opera performances weekly and wartime train journeys – many of those involved were convinced that the new opera was something important, not just for the company but for post-war British music. But this view was not unanimous. The original Captain Balstrode threw in the part when he found the music uncongenial and difficult. The casting of Joan Cross in the principal soprano role of Ellen Orford caused some resentment, especially since Elizabeth Abercrombie, another company soprano, was not offered a part at all. As Joan Cross said later, 'Ben wanted me to sing this piece – you know, he has very definite views about singers. I was administering the company and really stood back rather, didn't cast myself every day of the week. But he was adamant, and finally I did sing it. One or two sopranos were not too pleased.' Beyond all this, there was the sensitive matter of the 'conscientious objector' status of Britten and Pears, for whom the role of Grimes had been written. (At the première, a nervous stage staff were to mistake the audience's excited approval for a political demonstration and so they brought the curtain down prematurely.) Most fundamentally, there was nervousness about the choice of an untried British opera for the London reopening of the Wells: after all, the pre-war productions there of Nicholas Gatty's *Greysteel* and Lawrance Collingwood's *Macbeth* had sunk without trace. As Eric Crozier has said, some people expected a failure: 'There was indeed no tradition of writing opera; there was no tradition among audiences of wanting to see contemporary operas.'

The decision of Tyrone Guthrie and Joan Cross to mount *Peter Grimes* was indeed a bold one. Somehow their faith in the new opera carried rehearsals along. The première was, auspiciously, to be a young men's night: not only was there the composer himself, but the producer and conductor too, for the conductor Collingwood (who was shortly to retire) entrusted the direction of *Grimes* to the répétiteur Reginald Goodall. Little by little, even before the première, some of the doubters came around, even those of the chorus who found their music difficult. And though the orchestra too found their music hard to play, the first orchestral rehearsals made a big difference. The storm music, as Joan Cross remembered later, 'simply knocked you over totally'. Some musicians not associated with the Wells (one of whom was Michael Tippett) started coming in to listen at this stage; they went away impressed, booked seats for the first night and told their friends to do the same. But right up to the last moment, according to Joan Cross,

a lot of people in the company were, probably understandably, rather nervous. I was in my dressing room getting ready. And Tyrone Guthrie did the rounds to wish us all luck, came in, tapped me on the back and said, 'Whatever happens, we were quite right to do this piece.' It never occurred to me that there was any doubt in anyone's mind, *finally*, that it wouldn't catch on.

The story of *Peter Grimes* is fast-moving and dramatic. At the inquest on his apprentice, the fisherman Peter Grimes explains the boy's death as resulting from exposure at sea. He is exonerated but advised not to take another lad into his service. The object of Borough mistrust, Peter nevertheless has a friend in the widowed schoolmistress Ellen Orford (whom he hopes to marry when he has made enough money to become 'respectable') and two sympathetic acquaintances in Captain Balstrode and the pub landlady 'Auntie'. He does take another apprentice, John, but soon quarrels bitterly with Ellen over his ill-treatment of the boy. In an accident, John falls to his death from the cliff outside Grimes's hut and, now despairing and half-insane, Peter sails out at night to scuttle his boat and drown. As dawn comes, the Borough resumes its daily life, the tragedy washed away and quickly to be forgotten.

A vivid account of the première has been given by Imogen Holst.

No one in the audience will ever forget the excitement of that evening. Here, at last, was a real English opera that was going to live side by side with any of the great operas of the world. The drama in the music was utterly compelling from the first note to the last, and each of the characters had a musical personality. The story moved swiftly: there was no aimless hanging around, yet the singers sang real arias with memorable tunes that could be taken home and whistled. When the action needed the urgency of recitative, the sung conversations had all the directness and energy of their own native language. The huge orchestra never drowned the singers' words, yet when the east-coast storm arose the whole theatre was flooded with wave after wave of sound. Actors and audience were aware all the time of the cold, grey sea of Crabbe's poem: when a door at the back of the stage suddenly blew open at the height of the storm, Suffolk listeners sitting in the stalls could feel the north-east draught round their ankles. The music stretched beyond the boxed-in sides of the stage, and when the hostile crowds in the wings called out 'Peter Grimes! . . . Peter *Grimes!*', their voices sounded as if they were coming from far along the coast. In the fog of the terrible man-hunt, the poor demented fisherman seemed to grow in stature until he was no longer a separate individual: . . . he was bearing the burden of all those other outcasts who are rejected by their law-abiding neighbours because they are different from other people. When the tragedy had reached its quiet end and the opera was over, the listeners knew that they had been hearing a masterpiece and that nothing like this had ever happened before in English music. They stood up and shouted and shouted.

Next day, there were the papers. The *Daily Express* staff reporter characteristically went for 'human interest' and described the composer: 'A slim, curly-haired young man in evening dress stood for three hours at the back of the stalls in Sadler's Wells Theatre last night, too nervous to sit down. At the end he took an ovation from an audience containing some of the greatest names in music.' *The Times* critic was even more enthusiastic: 'It is a good omen for English opera that this first-fruit of peace should declare decisively that opera on the grand scale and in the grand manner can still be written.' In the *Daily Telegraph*, the review was by Ferruccio Bonavia. 'This opera has force, vitality, beauty,' he declared. '*Peter Grimes* equals and, in some respects, surpasses Mr Britten's previous essays in the choral and symphonic field.' Bonavia felt that the work had 'neither love-duet, nor hero' – perhaps a statement only half-true by modern standards – but found a 'haunting loveliness' and a 'rare and most valuable gift of characterisation'.

The critics of the Sunday papers, with more time and space to reflect upon the new opera, were no less favourable. In *The Observer*, William Glock noted that the subject had drawn from the composer 'orchestral writing of a darker and more menacing kind than he has had occasion to give us before' and was especially enthusiastic about the 'thrilling choruses such as the Round in the first act and the hymn of hate in the third, culminating in those tremendous shouts of "Grimes, Grimes"'. As for the church scene in Act II, involving Ellen, the apprentice and Peter, together with the off-stage chorus and the brilliantly apposite words of the Service, this he considered 'masterly ... such simple effects belong to genius'. Pears, Cross and Goodall were praised without reserve (as indeed they were in the other papers) and the review concluded with the words, 'Don't miss it.'

The Sunday Times did even better. In three separate articles

on the Sundays following the première, the doyen of English
music critics, Ernest Newman, then aged seventy-six, considered
Peter Grimes at length, describing it as 'a work of great originality
... the most important new work of the year'. He paid tribute
to the modification of Crabbe's original Grimes into a more
sympathetic and complex figure, and considered the apprentice's silent role (he never utters a word, sung or spoken, and the
only sound we hear from him is his scream as he falls to his
death) 'a stroke of genius'. He noted the orchestral interludes
'of great power and masterly musicianship ... and the superb
passacaglia', and summed up:

> The whole texture, musical and dramatic, of the opera is
> admirably unified, in spite of the many genres it employs,
> ranging from almost naked speech to music at its fullest power;
> but to listen to it in the right way the spectator must approach
> it from its own standpoint, not that of any previous operatic
> species.

Not everyone was quite as enthusiastic about *Peter Grimes*.
There were at least two dissenting voices, of whom the *Evening
News* critic Stephen Williams was one. 'A large abundance of
the spirit, over and above technique' was, he declared, 'the only
quality missing', and he found the story itself 'barren and re-
pellent'; yet he thought Britten's music 'very imaginative and
individual, with stretches of rather bony strength, a few moments
of heartfelt beauty ... when tenderness gushed out of the music
like water from a rock'. If Williams's review was partly unfavourable, clearly it was not damning: indeed three years later,
he wrote of *Grimes*, 'Its musical merits are undeniable'. The
comments by Geoffrey Sharp in *Music Review* (August 1945)
were far harsher. Sharp was the youthful owner and editor of
this journal and he took advantage of his position to lash out at
various targets, such as London orchestral standards or BBC
music policy, in a somewhat callow style. His opinion of *Peter
Grimes* is only quoted here because it reminds us of a scarcely
concealed hostility shown by some towards the composer: doubtless he was seen by these people as a young man of unorthodox
political views (socialist and pacifist), and private life, who now
after an 'easy war' was winning 'easy success'. Sharp wrote:

Opera virtually without melody, such as acts I and II of *Peter Grimes*, can be made tolerable only by first-rate production, lighting, singing and playing – none of which were in evidence at Sadler's Wells. In fact the whole effect was slapdash ... it is our belief that the music itself is poverty-stricken in regard to that quality which forms the mainspring of every convincing opera – a genuine ingrained emotional drive. Britten's score is arid and 'devilish smart'. He seems afraid to develop a lyrical vein and reluctant to express in his music any emotional conflict.

In 1979, Peter Pears could still recall this kind of adverse criticism: 'I remember, in *Music Review*, a man called Geoffrey Sharp, he disliked *Grimes* very much indeed. But it had too much impetus; you couldn't stop it. I mean, it was fairly clear that it was a masterpiece.' Two weeks after the première, Britten wrote in a letter to Imogen Holst:

> I am so glad that the opera came up to your expectations. I must confess that I am very pleased with the way that it seems to 'come over the footlights', and also with the way the audience takes it, and what is perhaps more, returns night after night to take it again! I think the occasion is actually a greater one than either Sadler's Wells or me. Perhaps it is an omen for English Opera in the future. Anyhow, I hope that many composers will take the plunge, and I hope also that they'll find, as I did, the water not quite so icy as expected!

What Peter Pears called the 'impetus' of *Peter Grimes* was to take the opera on a rapid conquest of the European and American opera houses. Within three years it had been translated into seven languages and received productions in Stockholm, Basle, Antwerp, Zurich, Tanglewood (under Leonard Bernstein), Milan, Hamburg, Mannheim, Berlin, Brno, Graz, Copenhagen, Budapest, New York (where *Time* devoted an article to 'Britain's Britten'), Stanford and Oldenburg. *Grimes* gave its composer near-immediate world-wide fame.

On 8 June 1945, the day after the première of *Peter Grimes*, the London newspapers carried not only their reviews of the opera but also those numerous items of daily news, advertisements and so on that serve to characterise a previous decade. 'Young men' born between June and September 1927 were reminded to register for National Service; housewives were told how to re-register with their new ration books and advised to get holiday sweets and chocolates before leaving home. Field-Marshal Montgomery received the Freedom of the City of Antwerp. 'Lord Haw-Haw' (William Joyce, who broadcast for the Nazis) was to be taken in custody to Brussels, but the Vichy French politician Pierre Laval was in Spain and thus out of the reach of the French authorities. There was a food shortage in London, though peaches were available (if only to the wealthy) at 5s 6d to 8s 6d each. A 5s-a-week children's allowance became payable for servicemen's families. Bakelite Plastics Ltd announced that 'furniture of the future will owe a great deal to Plastics'. The films *To Have and Have Not* (Bogart and Bacall) and *The Way to the Stars* (Redgrave and Mills) were reviewed. Vivien Leigh was at the Phoenix Theatre in Wilder's *The Skin of Our Teeth* and Phyllis Dixey was at the Whitehall in *While Parents Sleep* and *Peek-a-Boo*. Someone paid £72 for a silver tobacco box at Sotheby's, and Mackinlay's Scotch Whisky cost 25/9d a bottle.

This was the immediate context against which *Peter Grimes* began its career. Today the première of this opera already lies thirty-six years in the past. We should be able to see the event in a still clearer perspective than those contemporary commentators for we can view *Grimes* in the light of Britten's whole output and also in the context of subsequent musical history. In fact the 1945 critics were admirably perspicacious in seizing upon this new work as an augury of a major individual talent and a sign of promise for the future of English music. They rightly recognised its fluency of utterance, its command of wide-ranging moods, its dramatic immediacy and emotional force. They saw that it possessed not merely a well-shaped plot but also a correspondingly unified musical structure – something to be taken for granted in Mozart or Wagner (who achieve the same result by different means) but which is rare if not unknown in a relative novice; that Britten was a born musical dramatist was at once clear. All these qualities were valuable and largely explain the instant recognition of the opera's importance. Yet what sealed its success was surely something beyond. Here there was also a strikingly personal quality, expressed in a musical voice that was new. The *Peter Grimes* sound-scape was Britten's own because its feeling was so individual, strangely wounded perhaps yet defiant, tough and coolly intelligent. The passion and pain in *Grimes* are not of the cardboard-theatrical kind, but ring uncomfortably true. Its 'outsider' theme was of course to recur, differently, in later Britten operas like *Albert Herring* and *Death in Venice*, not surprisingly perhaps since in part it reflected the composer's own psychological make-up. Perhaps it is not going too far to suggest that *Grimes*'s impact was in part due to a quality not recognised as such in 1945, namely a quasi-autobiographical intensity.

2

A boy and his background
(1913–33)

I can-not grow;   I have no shadow to   run a-way from,

I on-ly play,   I on-ly play.

Hymn to St Cecilia

It was a happy stroke of fortune that gave Edward Benjamin Britten a birthday coinciding with the feast day of St Cecilia, the patron saint of music. More immediately, his home environment also directed his interests naturally towards music. His mother was an amateur singer and the secretary of the Lowestoft Choral Society, and it was in that Suffolk coastal town that he was born, at 21 Kirkley Cliff Road, on 22 November 1913.

His father, Robert Britten, was a dentist. He and his wife Edith had four children – Barbara, Robert, Beth and (belatedly and somewhat unexpectedly) Ben. A kindly man, Robert Britten was liked and respected in Suffolk. He also at times came to the financial aid of his relatives, so that bringing up four children left only limited funds for luxuries like travel. Nevertheless the family lived comfortably. There were servants in the house, good furniture, a large nursery, pictures and a piano in the drawing-room, but no gramophone, though it was early days for the mechanical reproduction of music. Britten is one of the last composers to have been brought up exclusively to the sound of 'live' music-making.

The first music he heard was his mother's singing. She had a clear soprano voice and at musical evenings held in the house she would sing German songs by Bach, Handel, Schubert or Schumann as well as arias from Mozart's or Wagner's operas. On the lighter side there were songs and ballads by Arthur Sullivan and Edward German, and English folk songs like 'Oh no, John' and 'The Keys of Heaven'. The celebrated soprano Lilian Stiles-Allen was one of many visiting singers who came as soloists to the Choral Society and were entertained in the house, and she made a lifelong admirer of her hostess's young son when she took him on her knee and sang 'Oh my sweet Hortense, she ain't good-looking but she's got good sense'.

Ben was a 'stiff, naïve little boy' – at least, that is how he was to look back on his childhood personality. He was intensely sensitive to music as a toddler and would cry with excitement when he heard it so that he could not be 'put down' to sleep when it was going on downstairs. But he seems to have been exceptionally happy at home (as the baby of the family he was rather spoiled) and he remained close to his family throughout his life. With his 'madly curly hair' (his own description), blue eyes and vivid, trusting smile, he was both adorable and adored. His personality was outgoing, as a young child; indeed he liked taking part in home amateur theatricals. A later shyness came with adolescence.

His first memory was of a sound, that of an exploding bomb, fortunately a rare occurrence in Suffolk. That was towards the end of the war. No doubt some would see this childhood moment as significant and point to his lifelong pacifism. But such recollections were soon put aside by a lively home life and, of course, his growing devotion to music. His mother started to teach him the piano, and the desire to write music for himself seems to have appeared almost at once, even before formal instruction began. One of his efforts was more visual than practical, 'like the Forth Bridge, in other words hundreds of dots all over the page connected by long lines all joined together in beautiful curves', which (to his great disappointment) his puzzled mother was unable to play. Then, with increasing keyboard fluency, he started to improvise, though not at first notate, miniature tone poems on the piano that were inspired by domestic events – his father setting off for a day in London, the making of a new friend or even a shipwreck. This was much more interesting than his prescribed practice, and when he had to work at scales he often read a novel at the same time, which he propped up on the music stand in front of him.

The world of boats and ships, and the sea itself, were very much part of his life, for the Britten house actually faced the North Sea and the sound of wind and waves, fishermen's voices and screeching herring-gulls was rarely absent. *Peter Grimes* and *Billy Budd*, *Noye's Fludde*, *The Golden Vanity* and the storm in *Saint Nicolas* owe much to this childhood background. But in the meantime some sort of formal technique was needed to shape the excited outpourings of a sensitive child. He later recalled: 'My later efforts luckily got away from these emotional inspirations and I began to write sonatas and quartets which were not connected in any direct way with life'. There were many of these: by the time he was fourteen he had composed ten piano sonatas, six string quartets, three piano suites, an oratorio and numerous songs.

In the meantime piano lessons continued. At eight he had gone for these to his school music mistress Ethel Astle, and he was soon able to accompany his mother and to play duets with the friendly organist of his local church, Charles Coleman. His string quartets must have owed something to his viola lessons begun at the age of ten with Mrs Audrey Alston, and at about this time he followed up his study of one of Stainer's musical textbooks (a birthday present from an uncle) with some 'proper' harmony lessons. It was Audrey Alston who in 1927 was to introduce him to his principal composition teacher, Frank Bridge.

As a day boy at his preparatory school, South Lodge, Ben worked hard – he was particularly good as a mathematician – and was good also at games, no small asset at a time when an exclusive passion for music would have been thought 'cissy' or at least 'cracked', schoolboy slang words of the time for 'effeminate' and 'eccentric'. As it was, he loved cricket, distinguished himself on the athletic field and actually became *victor ludorum*, the best all-round athlete. Because South Lodge was only five minutes' walk from his home, he was something of an exception as a day boy in a school really meant for boarders. But he attended from early morning until bedtime. Since the school timetable left little if any leisure, much of his composition was done at home first thing in the morning or last thing at night, even in bed.

There were a young composer's piano pieces, sometimes minuscule in dimension but carefully marked with the exciting Italian terms of expression that he found in his Stainer text book. '*Rubato moltissimo*' clearly marked some especially romantic moment; the rare '*mancando*' might appear for 'dying away' instead of the usual word *morendo*. And the youthful linguist had his lapses, as when French and Italian cheerfully mixed in the '*dolce et piano*' marking of a 1923 Waltz in B major. But mostly the work was meticulous. Expression marks and those of phrasing and articulation were always there; so was the pianist's pedalling. When he wrote for organ, he marked in the stop changes, and similarly when he composed for stringed instruments every detail of bowing was inserted.

Among the young Britten's songs were settings of Longfellow, Tennyson, Shelley, Kipling and of course Shakespeare. He even used a few French texts – indeed at the age of fourteen, under some Debussy and Ravel influence, he was to compose a group of songs for soprano with orchestra to poems by Victor Hugo and Paul Verlaine. There were passages from the Bible, forerunners of future sacred works. Even more prophetic, this time of the future opera composer, were settings of fragments of plays. The nine-year-old chose some of his best songs and had them bound up in a single volume as a present to his parents. One of these was a twelve-bar setting of Longfellow's 'Beware!', a description of a 'maiden fair' who is evidently also a *femme fatale*: the text ends with the words 'trust her not, she's fooling thee, Beware!'. The music, 'by E. B. Britten', alternates tonic and subdominant chords hypnotically in F minor until the cautionary last line brings a sudden chromaticism and a somewhat surprising final major-minor alternation. The sense of drama in miniature is striking; and so is the early use of a later Britten 'trademark', the repetition of significant words.

In the meantime he shared in the happy home life of an educated middle-class family in provincial England. The Brittens went to St John's Church every Sunday. Ben enjoyed the fêtes and fairs and obstacle races, riding his bike and playing

tennis, taking part in amateur dramatics or swimming parties
– the latter not in comfortable urban pools but in the rough and
usually cold North Sea. There are family 'snaps' that somehow
represent the time and place: the four-year-old in white socks
sitting playing with a toy ship on a leopard-skin rug; the lad of
seven outdoors, perhaps on the 'front', with shoes that look too
big for him, rumpled socks, short trousers over bony knees and
holding anxiously on to a floppy hat. A more formal eleven-
year-old, in the garden, sports a wing collar, waistcoat, straw
hat and polished boots, smiling happily. One family picture,
taken on the lawn with friends, shows a summer tea party with
the adults at table and the children on the grass; the tea things,
lace tablecloth, parasol, deck and basket chairs, white dresses
and cricket flannels all speak clearly of an England that is now
half a century past.

So far (in those prep school days) most of the young Britten's
experience of live music had been confined to what was available
in Lowestoft. But he read a lot of music scores. When the family
had a day in London (about a hundred and thirty miles away)
he was usually given three and sixpence, and with that he could
go and browse at length in the music shop run by the publisher
Augener. The browsing process allowed his eagerly questing
mind to absorb much that was stimulating and useful; and at
the end of it he could make a choice of a score or two to take
home and study, either silently in his head or at the piano.
Usually he chose miniature scores of orchestral music.

His interest in orchestral music, and indeed in modern music,
started to develop strongly when he was about twelve. He found
Gustav Holst's part-song 'The Song of the Ship-builders' (1910)
in his local music shop and liked its unfamiliar harmonies and
rhythmical vitality. He also managed to hear the same composer's *The Planets*, finding that exciting, and also Ravel's
String Quartet. At the Norwich Triennial Festival of 1924 he
heard the composer Frank Bridge conduct his orchestral suite
The Sea (1911) and, in his own words, was 'knocked sideways'.
It was thrilling to see a real, live composer performing his own
music. The Britten style, which he later described as 'sort of
early nineteenth century', now began to get progressively more
adventurous: 'I started writing in a much freer harmonic idiom.'

An ambitious orchestral Overture in B flat minor (not the easiest of keys with its five flats!) was written when he was twelve, ninety-one pages of score in nine days at the end of a school summer term despite the pressures of exams and cricket. This seems to have been the point at which his parents realised that they must find him a composition teacher. When Frank Bridge came to East Anglia, he used to stay with his friend Audrey Alston, who was Ben's viola teacher. Since *The Sea* had been a considerable success in 1924, Bridge was invited to compose a new orchestral piece for the next Norwich Festival in 1927. He duly arrived with a colourful rhapsody called *Enter Spring*. On this occasion the young Britten was taken by Mrs Alston to meet him.

It was a happy encounter, for Frank Bridge was to become Britten's 'prime mentor'. Long afterwards, in 1966, he wrote a tribute to Bridge which is worth quoting at length.

We got on splendidly, and I spent the next morning with him going over some of my music.... From that moment I used to go regularly to him, staying with him in Eastbourne or in London, in the holidays from my prep school. Even though I was barely in my teens, this was immensely serious and professional study; and the lessons were mammoth. I remember one that started at half past ten, and at tea-time Mrs Bridge came in and said, 'Really, Frank, you must give the boy a break.' Often I used to end these marathons in tears; not that he was beastly to me, but the concentrated strain was too much for me. I was perhaps too young to take in so much at one time, but I found later that a good deal of it had stuck firmly ... Bridge insisted on the absolutely clear relationship of what was in my mind to what was on the paper. I used to get sent to the other side of the room; Bridge would play what I'd written and demand if it was what I'd really meant. He taught me to think and feel through the instrument I was writing for: he was most naturally an instrumental composer, and as a superb viola player he thought instrumentally ... I badly needed his kind of strictness. It was just the right treatment for me.

Over thirty years later, Britten was still to say (with a striking generosity) that he did not feel he had yet come up to the technical standards set for him as a boy by this teacher to whom he felt he owed so much.

It was not only in his formal lessons in music that he learned and benefited from Frank Bridge. 'It was, of course,' he wrote later, 'the first time I had seen how an artist lived. I heard conversations which centred around the arts; I heard the latest poems discussed, and the latest trends in painting and sculpture. Bridge ... had a circle of highly cultured friends, many of whom were artists and musicians.' There were car trips, too, that took in the 'tucked-away little villages' of southern England with their churches, and the Bridges even took him over to Paris for a few days so that his exciting contacts with French music and literature took on a new dimension. Politically, the older musician and the young boy shared a then unconventional pacifism. Bridge's Piano Sonata had been written in memory of a friend killed in the war; over thirty years later, and in the shadow of another war, Britten's own *War Requiem* was to bear a similar dedication.

Quite apart from music, Ben was an unusually thoughtful and sensitive boy, even at the 'puppy' stage of prep school. He himself was later to speak of the extra-thin skin that makes an artist an artist and which sometimes makes him do unpopular things. As head prefect at South Lodge, he fought against bullying and offended the masters by an end-of-term essay against blood sports (an important part of English country life) and advocating pacifism. It is also thought-provoking to note that in his *Quatre chansons françaises*, the orchestral song group of 1928, the fourteen-year-old composer set some very disillusioned poetry of Verlaine.

To go from a preparatory to a public school was the natural step for a boy with Britten's background. Accordingly in September 1928 he entered Gresham's School, at Holt in Norfolk, some thirty-five miles from his home. His parents took him by car and left him to wander around the playing fields and get his bearings. Almost the first person he met was the school music master. But this contact was not auspicious. 'So you are the little boy who likes Stravinsky!' was the greeting he received, and it was accompanied by a frown rather than the welcoming smile that might be expected from a teacher acquiring a talented pupil. Later, he was to write with a trace of bitterness, 'At my public school my musical education was practically non-existent.' The other boys expressed 'vocal and energetic surprise' when they found him reading orchestral scores in bed: presumably the energy was expressed in some sort of rough treatment.

Still, Gresham's was not all bad. Caning and compulsory military training were not the order of the day, as in most schools at the time, and there was a decent debating society which encouraged the boys to think for themselves and express their views. Probably Ben was sometimes homesick, for unlike most of the other boys, he had never been a boarder before. But at least there was a choir and an orchestra. The school magazine for the Christmas term of 1929 noted that, as a viola player, 'E. B. Britten proved a very reliable musician in ensemble work', and later his piano playing was thought 'of a high standard' and such as to show promise that 'he should go far'. He now had piano lessons from Harold Samuel in London, and he continued (at least in the school holidays) to work at composition with Frank Bridge.

Britten did not stay at Gresham's for the usual three- or four-year period. Instead he left at the age of sixteen, after what Peter Pears has called 'two uneasy years'. One is tempted to think that the tough environment of an English boarding school (albeit one far more liberal than many), together with the trauma of adolescence, was in some way unsettling and unnerving. The world of emotional and intellectual security that he had known at home and at his prep school had gone, never to return. Much of his later music was to exhibit nostalgia for that age of innocence.

The decision to make music his career had been easily reached. Since his earliest days, he had shown a passionate commitment to the subject and a keen ambition to pursue it. His parents loyally backed him; and the musical establishment, in the shape of the Royal College of Music in London, did the same by awarding him an Open Scholarship for composition. Nevertheless the choice of an artistic profession caused some raised eyebrows in his native Lowestoft. That the local dentist's son should play the piano and compose was admirable; but surely, when one looked to the future and the serious matter of earning a living, one had to turn to a 'proper profession' like medicine, or the law – or even teaching, like Ben's elder brother Robert. In his last summer at Lowestoft the young musician was playing tennis with a few friends and found himself being asked what career he intended to follow now that he had left school (this was in August 1930). 'I told them I intended to be a composer. They were amazed! "Yes, but what *else*?" ' He simply could not get it across to them that composing music was more than a hobby.

Britten's expectations of the Royal College of Music were high, and this was natural enough in the circumstances. All the time he had been at Gresham's School he had looked forward to full-time music in London as a kind of goal; he was full of creative energy and composing as freely as ever. (Even when without manuscript paper, and ill in the Gresham's sanatorium during his last year, he drew the stave lines on ordinary paper and composed the eight-part vocal *Hymn to the Virgin* – initially in B flat minor instead of its present A minor.) But perhaps he should have been warned, for even on the occasion of his RCM scholarship examination someone was heard to ask, 'What is an English public schoolboy doing writing music of this kind?' The remark was overheard by John Ireland, the examiner who was in favour of his getting the award and who in fact was to become his composition professor. The other two examiners were Ralph Vaughan Williams and the now-forgotten Sidney Waddington: one hopes that it was not Vaughan Williams who failed to recognise at once a major young talent.

In the event, Britten's period of study at the Royal College of Music was not as productive as he expected, and not especially happy. His composition professor, John Ireland, though kindly, seemed to him 'gloomy' and evidently taught him little. He very quickly became impatient of the elementary aural training that was offered in classes, feeling that he was wasting time doing tests which simply did not test him. In his three years at the college, only one of his compositions was performed there: this was his chamber Sinfonietta of 1932, and even this had been played outside before the RCM heard it in March 1933. Frank Bridge tried to persuade the college to perform two 'choral psalms' by its brilliant student, arguing reasonably that a student composer should have a chance to hear what he had written, since 'without aural experience it was difficult to link notes and sounds'. The answer, from Vaughan Williams, was that the singers weren't up to the standard of difficulty of the music, to which Bridge retorted that they ought to be. But it was to no avail.

However, Bridge (to whom Britten had dedicated the Sinfonietta) was himself still available. He and the young Britten used to go to concerts together, sometimes at the BBC where Bridge himself quite frequently conducted. The BBC's public concerts provided several opportunities to hear exciting new music. On 8 February 1933 Britten heard Schoenberg conduct his orchestral Variations and even met the Austrian composer briefly. A month later he found three excerpts from Berg's *Wozzeck* 'thoroughly sincere and moving'. A few days after that there was a Stravinsky chamber concert, while on 23 March he heard Webern conduct Mahler's 'lovely Fourth Symphony ... like a lovely spring day'. In November 1933 he heard more Schoenberg: 'The joy of the evening was *Pierrot Lunaire*, with Erika Wagner as a divine reciter (amazingly accurate). But what a work! The imagination and technique of it. I revelled in the romanticism of it.' By contrast, the Royal College of Music did its best to deny him access to such provocative and controversial modern music: his request that its library should purchase a score of *Pierrot Lunaire* was refused. (*Pierrot* was in any case hardly new: it was composed in 1912.)

Britten's tastes, at the age of twenty, were now changing rapidly, as he absorbed more and more varied musical experiences. Frank Bridge's approach to composition was in some ways Germanic, and this no longer wholly satisfied him. His early enthusiasm for Beethoven and Brahms had certainly diminished, though he still loved Mozart and Schubert; as for his more recent discoveries, these were not confined to the newer music, and Purcell and the English madrigalists also excited his imagination. He still had informal lessons with Bridge during his time at the Royal College of Music. But now he sometimes rebelled at the older composer's strictures, based as they were upon techniques that he could no longer always accept. 'Is that chord what you really mean?' Bridge would ask him, and he would retort, 'Yes, it *is*.'

Nevertheless, Britten's years at the Royal College had many positive features. They gave him the chance to meet other young musicians and exchange ideas. Under the guidance of his teacher Arthur Benjamin he worked quite hard at his piano playing and passed the Performers' Associateship of the Royal College of Music diploma in December 1933; and he also won the Ernest Farrar Composition Prize worth seven pounds. More importantly, he was awarded a travelling composition scholarship which seems to have been an offshoot of the prestigious Mendelssohn Scholarship. This gave him what seemed like an inspired idea: having heard Alban Berg's opera *Wozzeck* in a concert performance, he wanted to use this scholarship money to travel to Vienna and study with Berg. But though Frank Bridge supported his request, the college authorities were against it and the idea fell through. Serial or 'twelve-note' music – the idiom of Schoenberg, Berg and Webern – was distrusted and disliked in England: thus Berg was thought of as potentially 'not a good influence'. Britten's parents, too, were unconvinced by his Viennese plans. 'They had been disturbed,' he wrote long afterwards, 'by traits of rebelliousness and unconventionality which I had shown in my later school days.' Both he and they inevitably suffered the gentle, nagging pain of those years in which a brilliant, happy child grows up and seeks his own way. Nevertheless the Britten family unity remained strong. While at the Royal College the young composer lived in the same boarding-house as his sister Beth, and then after leaving the college he used his travelling scholarship money to travel as a tourist with his mother to Europe.

It is curious to realise how few Britten compositions were actually performed in all this period of his childhood, schooldays and studentship. A young composer really does need to hear his work as *sound* to be sure that what he has put down on paper corresponds to what he has heard in his head. Of course Britten could play his own piano music, and his mother or some other musician could sing his songs, but it was a very different matter when it came to elaborate ensemble pieces with their complex textures and tone-colour mixes – like his Sinfonietta for ten instruments or the unaccompanied choral variations of winter 1932–33 called *A Boy was Born*. As we know, Frank Bridge made this point. But one cannot help suspecting that his teachers generally, both at school and (shamefully) at the Royal College of Music also, thought of free composition in much the same way as they regarded harmony and counterpoint exercises: as 'paper music' in which the teacher merely noted observance or otherwise of accepted rules, and in which the assessment of quality was related only to known techniques. But this is inadequate for a real composer, who must create his own language upon the basis of those various techniques and stylistic features which his individual talent has caused him to adopt. A passage from Bach would sound, and indeed *be*, incorrect in Beethoven – or, for that matter, Britten. This makes the teaching of composition difficult if not impossible for the merely academic musician. As a real composer, John Ireland might have helped Britten, by recognising the nature of his student's developing language and using his greater experience to help him towards its realisation. Later, Ireland was to say that he recognised in his student 'one of the finest musical brains the college had seen for many years'. Nevertheless Britten, as as we have seen, found little that was stimulating in his composition lessons. And where he could have learned much, by having the opportunity to hear his own music, the college failed him.

Still, there was a Britten motet, *New Prince, New Pomp*, for soprano and chorus, that was performed in 1929. A carol, 'I saw three ships', was sung in 1931 at his local church, St John's in Lowestoft. In London during the college years the young composer was lucky to find an outlet in the Macnaghten-Lemare Concerts that took place in the Ballet Club (later the Mercury Theatre) at Notting Hill Gate. His one-movement Phantasy for string quintet, doubtless inspired by the Cobbett Competition which required works with this form and title, was performed there on 12 December 1932 (it was also broadcast on 17 February 1933, as were his Three Part-Songs for women's voices to texts by de la Mare). It was at these concerts also that the Sinfonietta (his 'official' Opus 1) was played on 31 January 1933. Another Phantasy, this time for oboe and string trio, received still wider recognition. Written in the autumn of 1932, it was played by Leon Goossens and members of the International String Quartet and made a considerable impression at the Festival of the International Society for Contemporary Music held in Florence in April 1934. According to Ferruccio Bonavia, writing in the first edition of Bacharach's *Musical Companion* published in the same year, this piece was acclaimed both in London and Florence as 'a work of distinct originality'; and in the same book Edwin Evans noted with reference to the Phantasy, 'at the moment much is expected of a very young composer, Benjamin Britten'.

The critical recognition must have been welcome. At the same time, Britten discovered how sensitive he was to adverse criticism – or at least to the kind of critical comment which he felt to be inaccurate, inept and misleading. A notice by a journalist called 'C.D.' in *Music Lover* upset him by its comments on his Three Part-Songs of 1932. This critic called them 'good from one who, I believe, is only 19; even though they were reminiscent in a quite peculiar degree of Walton's latest songs which were heard recently elsewhere'. Years later, in 1952, Britten still smarted under this patronising half-praise. In an article called 'Variations on a Critical Theme' he wrote that this review of the songs 'damned them entirely' (not really true) and called them 'obvious copies of Walton's three *Façade* Songs' (also not altogether true).'. . . anyone who is interested,' he went on, 'can see for himself that this is silly nonsense. The Walton songs are brilliant and sophisticated in the extreme – mine could scarcely have been more childlike and naïve, with not a trace of parody throughout.' But what mattered really was less that the criticism was incompetent than that he had found himself to be easily wounded where discussion of his music was concerned. 'It is easy to imagine the damping effect of this first notice on a young composer. I was furious and dismayed because I could see there was not a word of truth in it. I was also considerably discouraged.'

But what had happened to undermine Britten's confidence? Did he really care about the reaction of an unknown journalist to his music after one hearing? Why be 'considerably discouraged' when, as he himself said, there was 'not a word of truth' in the criticism? It was hardly logical. But his reaction was real and characteristic. Later he was to speak of an artist's 'extra sensitivity'; and he was always to suffer from it where his music was concerned.

3

Young professionalism: Auden and Pears (1934–39)

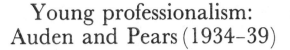

Albert Herring, Act II

Britten completed his studies at the Royal College of Music at the end of 1933, and, although he had held a scholarship for composition, his final qualification (as we have seen) was not in that subject but in piano playing. He was proud of his new diploma, sending his parents a postcard containing the brief message, in block capitals, 'BENJAMIN BRITTEN A.R.C.M. Much Love.' He was pleased, too, to be able to use his ability as a solo pianist in occasional concerts. One of these was given on 9 July 1934 in St John's Church at Lowestoft, with the organist Charles Coleman. The programme was ambitious, ranging from Bach via Mozart and Tchaikovsky to Schoenberg's Op. 19 Piano Pieces and a movement, 'arr. B.B.', from Frank Bridge's suite *The Sea* which, being called 'Moonlight', uncannily anticipates Britten's own future sea interlude of that name in *Peter Grimes*. Of this occasion, the young pianist wrote in his diary:

> Quite full – very hot – I play most of the time in just tennis shirt & trousers. We do Schumann conc. – 1st mov. I play slow mov. of Beethoven Appassionata, and 6 small Schönberg pieces, & then with Org. my arr. of F.B.'s 'Moonlight'. Then we struggle thro' Tschaikov. 1st mov. – Mr Coleman plays

Bach E min. pre. & fug., I do L'isle Joyeux and both finish
off with Mozart E♭ Symph. Finale – my arr.

The Beethoven sonata and Debussy (*L'isle joyeuse*) may have
been his ARCM examination pieces, and of course he would
have had to play the whole sonata for the examiners; the fact
that he was equal to these and able also to 'struggle thro'' the
first movement of Tchaikovsky's First Concerto, cascading octaves and all, makes one wish that he had publicly played more
of the solo repertory later. But this aspect of his music-making
was virtually to cease before very long.

It was towards composition above all that Britten directed his
energies upon leaving the Royal College, and it was from composing that he was to set about earning his living. But first, as 1934
began, he took time to look around him and to travel. The year
was divided between spells of composition and continental trips.
He was encouraged to hear the first performance of *A Boy was
Born*, a broadcast by the BBC Singers that took place on 23
February. It was at this time, too, that he first met Peter Pears,
the tenor singer who was later to become his lifelong companion;
Pears, who had just joined the BBC Singers, was doubtless more
conscious of their brief encounter in a broadcasting studio than
was Britten, for the young composer (three years his junior) was
already getting a 'name'. But it was not until 1937 that they
were to become friends. In the meantime, February 1934 also
saw the completion of Britten's *Simple Symphony*, a work for
string orchestra based on piano music and songs written before
he was thirteen. His attachment to such early pieces is significant, as are the rather naïve titles of the movements, 'Boisterous
Bourrée', 'Playful Pizzicato', 'Sentimental Saraband' and 'Frol-
icsome Finale'. One has the impression of a young man whose
intellectual assurance was not yet matched by a corresponding
emotional maturity. That impression is reinforced by the title of
an unfinished string quartet, 'Go play, boy, play', containing a
movement called 'Alla Burlesca (ragging)'. Still, the musical
skills were assured enough, and even though he had received no
formal training as a conductor he directed the first performance
of the *Simple Symphony* in Norwich on 6 March. A month later
he was in Italy for the successful première of his Phantasy Quar-

tet at the Florence ISCM Festival on 5 April. Sadly, his father died on the following day and on receiving the news he left Italy on 9 April and hurried back to Lowestoft.

The year 1934 also saw the composition of what was to be his only substantial work for piano solo, the 'Holiday Diary' which he dedicated to his piano teacher Arthur Benjamin: its four movements, called 'Early morning bathe', 'Sailing', 'Funfair' and 'Night', again have boyish titles, but the harmonic adventurousness of 'Night' has nothing English-provincial about it. The schoolboy that remained inside the rather self-consciously sophisticated young composer must also have enjoyed writing a set of twelve children's songs called *Friday Afternoons*. These were actually composed over a period, between 1933 and 1935, and although not his first music for boys' voices (the Three Part-Songs of 1932 are 'for boys' or women's voices' and *A Boy was Born* has boy as well as adult singers) they were to have many successors. *Friday Afternoons* were dedicated to his brother Robert and the boys whom Robert Britten taught as the headmaster of Clive House School at Prestatyn on the rugged north coast of Wales, and the composer went down to stay there for a few days. In October and November 1934 he was once again abroad, taking his widowed mother to Europe; this was a holiday made possible partly by the money of the RCM travelling scholarship. Edith Britten must have appreciated her son's kindness, and doubtless he too enjoyed taking her to new and exciting places like Basle, Salzburg, Vienna, Munich and finally Paris. He was also with her at home in Lowestoft in December, presumably for Christmas. But London, where his sister Beth was still living, was necessarily his professional base. His music was now being performed there and making some impact. *A Boy was Born*, dedicated to his father, was given a public performance at a Macnaghten-Lemare concert on 17 December; and on the very same day the violinist Henri Temianka and Betty Humby (the future Lady Beecham) played at London's Wigmore Hall three movements of a new and as yet unfinished Suite for Violin and Piano which he had started (though nominally on holiday) in Vienna the previous month.

1935 found Britten settling in to something like a disciplined routine of professional work. He found himself a flat at 559

Finchley Road, London, where his sister Beth kept house for him, and he set about earning his living. He was to write in 1946:

> I was determined to do it through composition: it was the only thing I cared about and I was sure it was possible. My first opportunity was the chance of working in a film company. This was much to my taste although it meant a great deal of hard work. I had to work quickly, to force myself to work when I didn't want to, and to get used to working in all kinds of circumstances. The film company I was working for was not a big commercial one; it was a documentary company and had little money. I had to write scores ... for not more than six or seven players, and to make those instruments make all the effects that each film demanded. I also had to be ingenious and try to imitate ... the natural sounds of everyday life. I well remember the mess we made in the studio one day when trying to fit an appropriate sound to shots of a large ship unloading in a dock. We had pails of water which we slopped everywhere, drain-pipes with coal slipping down them, ... whistles and every kind of paraphernalia we could think of.

The film company in question was the GPO Film Unit, a department controlled by the Post Office and directed artistically by John Grierson. Between 1935 and 1939 Britten was to contribute music to eighteen films made by this company. Their titles obviously relate to the Post Office's activities – *The King's Stamp, Night Mail, How the Dial Works* – but the treatment of these subjects was often highly imaginative. For the story of *The King's Stamp*, a special design for George V's silver jubilee issue, Britten scored for flute (or piccolo), clarinet, percussion and piano duet. In *Coal Face*, with its Welsh mining background, he used voices as well as instruments, while he gave the Scotland-bound express of *Night Mail* vividly rhythmical music for clarinet, trumpet and string orchestra. The percussionist James Blades remembers that the recording session for *Night Mail* gave the musicians 'plenty to keep them busy and interested'.

In both *Coal Face* and *Night Mail* Britten was fortunate in having the literary collaboration of the poet W. H. Auden. Wystan Auden was to be one of his most important artistic associates, and an influential friend, during a period of about seven years. He was six years older than Britten and had by coincidence gone to the same public school, Gresham's; at Christ Church, Oxford, he edited *Oxford Poetry* and was to find his own poetic voice very young. Auden's directness and urgency of language made an instant impact upon the reader, as did his sense of struggle: 'war between classes, between parties, between members – war between life and death', as one writer has put it. Britten was to describe him later as 'a powerful, revolutionary person. He was very much anti-bourgeois and that appealed.' Auden's idea of 'parable art . . . which shall teach man to unlearn hatred and learn love' also found a ready response in the pacifist-minded composer.

The first meeting between Britten and Auden took place on 4 July 1935, when the film producer and director Basil Wright drove Britten down to the prep school near Malvern where Auden was teaching. Auden had already been asked to script *Coal Face* and *Night Mail*, for which Britten was to provide music. The director for *Coal Face* was Cavalcanti and the film, made in 1936, contained Britten's first setting of an Auden text: this was the poem 'Oh lurcher-loving collier, black as night,' sung by women's voices. In *Night Mail*, directed by John Grierson, Auden provided short, exciting lines suggesting the motion of a great express passing anonymously through the sleeping countryside, while for a train approaching through a tunnel in *Coal Face* Britten ingeniously reversed the sound track of a cymbal clash to produce a crescendo.

In November 1935 Ralph Hawkes, of Boosey & Hawkes, had given Britten a publishing contract. Mr Hawkes showed a steady faith in the young composer, though his firm made little money from his music at first; in the meantime Britten offered a gesture of gratitude in the dedication of a new orchestral song cycle called *Our Hunting Fathers*. This was to be written, in collaboration with Auden, in the summer of 1936. At the beginning of that year, Britten took stock of his career in a diary entry worth quoting at length:

1936 finds me infinitely better off in all ways than did the beginning of 1935; it finds me earning my living – with

occasionally something to spare – at the GPO film Unit under
John Grierson & Cavalcanti, writing music & supervising
sounds for films (this one TPO Night Mail) at the rate of £5
per week, but owing to the fact that I can claim no performing
rights (it being Crown property) with the possibility of it
being increased to £10 per week or £2 per day; writing very
little, but with the possibility & ideas for writing a lot of
original music, as I am going under an agreement with Boosey
& Hawkes for a £3 a week guarantee of royalties; having a
lot of success but not a staggering amount of performances,
the reputation (even for bad) growing steadily; having a bad
inferiority complex in company of brains like Basil Wright,
Wystan Auden & William Coldstream; being fortunate in
friends like Mr & Mrs Frank Bridge, Henry Boys, Basil
Reeve ... being comfortably settled in a pleasant, tho' cold,
flat in West Hampstead with Beth, with whom I get on very
well; doing much housework but with prospect of having a
woman in more than twice a week in evenings & once in
mornings. So for 1936.

(Henry Boys and Basil Reeve were close to Britten at the time:
Boys was to be the dedicatee of Britten's Violin Concerto of 1939
and later worked for the English Opera Group.)

But 1936 was not only crucial in Britten's career as a composer; it was also a year in which he found himself forced to
come to terms with his adult personality. It was not an easy
time, for as Peter Pears has said, 'as he grew up he became
increasingly disappointed' in the realities of adult life. He was
sometimes shocked by his less inhibited contemporaries. Auden
in particular disturbed him as he was a fairly promiscuous and
unashamed homosexual. Everything in Britten's upbringing
conditioned him to disapprove; but he too was conscious of a
homosexual orientation, while Auden was someone for whom
he had considerable intellectual respect. As for the poet and his
generally homosexual circle, they thought Britten emotionally
backward and rather mischievously felt that it was time he
outgrew the world of funfairs and early morning bathes (titles
in the piano 'Holiday Diary') and discovered material for more
interesting diary entries. Auden wrote a poem including the

lines 'For my friend Benjamin Britten, composer, I beg/That fortune send him soon a passionate affair.' One evening Christopher Isherwood and Basil Wright, dining with Britten, said to each other when he was out of the room: 'Well, have we convinced Ben he's queer, or haven't we?' Britten was both attracted and repelled by this (for him) *louche* world. Though Auden introduced him to Rimbaud's poetry (telling him of that brilliant boy's affair with Verlaine) and he was later to set some of *Les Illuminations*, Rimbaud was also, as Pears tells us, 'the young sensitive innocent lost in great cities with whom it was easy for Britten to identify himself'. Auden, though temperamentally quite different from Britten, understood his deep nostalgia for lost innocence. Later, it was for (and *to*, and *about*) Britten that he wrote the *Hymn to St Cecilia* with its poignant lament: 'O weep, child, weep, O weep away the stain,/Lost innocence who wish'd your lover dead,/Weep for the lives your wishes never led.'

Britten's homosexuality was never publicly discussed in his lifetime, even after the English law on the matter had changed. He was, after all, entirely un-Bohemian and even Puritan, seeming quite consciously to have sought to live 'decently' and free of scandal. Only after his death, when this delicate matter had been broached in the press and on radio, did it receive a kind of *imprimatur* from the man to whom the composer was in a sense married for forty years, Peter Pears. In a television biography broadcast in 1980, he spoke of their relationship as one of 'passionate devotion, faith and love'; a few months earlier he had described their relationship to me as 'wonderful, glorious, marvellous'. But he added that the cult word 'gay' was never in Britten's vocabulary.

Did Britten ever think of Auden's influence on himself when in later years he set Peter Quint's words in *The Turn of the Screw* ('I seek a friend –/Obedient to follow where I lead,/Slick as a juggler's mate to catch my thought/... And in that hour/"The ceremony of innocence is drowned"'), or those of the Tempter in *The Prodigal Son* ('Imagine, imagine,/What you are missing/... High living, secret delights,/And beauty, beauty/To kindle your senses,/While you are young, still young,/... Act out your desires!')? According to Donald Mitchell, Britten's publisher and

literary executor, the diaries the young composer kept from
1928–38 tell us something of the 'ambiguous relationship
between private and public life'; and he adds that 'the friction
generated by the private/public dichotomy is a fruitful one'.
Mitchell reminds us in this context of the homoerotic theme of
the composer's last opera, *Death in Venice*. 'O the taste of knowledge,' the writer Aschenbach cries as he awakens from a Dionysiac dream of the beautiful boy Tadzio. 'The opera was, in some
sort of way, a summing up of what he felt,' Peter Pears has said.
'At the end, Aschenbach asks ... what it is he has spent his life
searching for. Knowledge? A lost innocence? And must the pursuit of beauty, of love, lead only to chaos? All questions Ben
constantly asked himself.'

In 1936, then, Wystan Auden figured large in the life of the
twenty-two-year-old composer, both personally and artistically
– if indeed it is helpful to make the distinction in Britten's case,
where work and private life were virtually one. On 2 January
the two men met for a preliminary discussion of the orchestral
song cycle *Our Hunting Fathers* commissioned by the committee
of the Norwich Triennial Festival who, it seemed, wished to
encourage a gifted young composer with East Anglian associ-
ations. Its subject was 'animals' – animals as pests, pets or crea-
tures to be killed for pleasure – and it was probably chosen by
Auden, though it had the kind of provocative, schoolboyish
unconventionality that appealed also to Britten. Of the five
poems in the cycle, the three central ones were not by Auden,
two being anonymous and the third by the seventeenth-century
poet Thomas Ravenscroft; but the prologue and epilogue were
Auden's own. By March Britten had his text. Down at Friston,
in Sussex, he spent a wet morning indoors with Frank
Bridge, writing in his diary, 'I show him Auden's stuff for me
and he is impressed. Also find he is very sympathetic towards
my socialistic inclinations.' Possibly this was Auden's influence
too: the poet was a kind of Christian Marxist, though never a
Communist Party member. Britten's diary entry about Bridge
goes on: 'in fact we are in complete agreement over all – except
Mahler! – though he admits he is a great thinker.' The enthusiasm for Mahler, then little played in England, was fairly new:
the composer Lennox Berkeley has told me how Britten once

called on him in great excitement to play the Ninth Symphony, carried as a pile of 78 rpm records under his arm. Not much Mahler was avilable then on disc, but passages in *Our Hunting Fathers* suggest that Britten knew, at least from the score, the 'Schattenhaft' ('shadowy') scherzo movement in the Seventh Symphony. (So does the central scherzo of the *Sinfonia da Requiem* four years later, in the same D minor – a favourite key for Mahler and Britten alike.)

Our Hunting Fathers had its first performance on 25 September 1936 at Norwich; the soprano soloist was Sophie Wyss and Britten conducted the London Philharmonic Orchestra. It was 'uncomfortable music ... spiky, exact and not at all cosy', Pears has written, 'all part of a brilliant twenty-two-year-old's revolt against the stuffy and sloppy'. According to the critic Scott Goddard, writing ten years later in *British Music of our Time*, it

> amused the sophisticated, scandalised those among the gentry who caught Auden's words, and left musicians dazzled at so much talent, uneasy that it should be expended on so arid a subject, not knowing whether to consider Britten's daring style as the outcome of courage or foolhardiness ... (it) made an impression of class-consciousness ... it connects him with what was then the most forward-looking group of artists in England.

Britten's mother 'disapproved very thoroughly' of parts of the music, he wrote, but he himself was pleased with the work – 'I am exhilarated at having finished Hunting Fathers' – and after a second (broadcast) performance in London with the BBC Symphony Orchestra under Adrian Boult he was to add, 'it's my Op. 1 alright'. Admittedly the work was then shelved and was not performed again until 1951; but it had made an impression as his first performed work for full orchestra.

Of course, Britten had other musical irons in the fire besides his work with Auden. In April 1936 he was at the Barcelona Festival of the International Society for Contemporary Music for the first complete public performance of his Suite for Violin and Piano, which Antonio Brosa and he had broadcast from London (on the BBC National Programmme) on 13 March. (The *Radio Times* carried pictures of the two artists, describing the Suite as 'distinctly "modern" '.) This Barcelona visit brought him into congenial contact with Lennox Berkeley, ten years older but seeming like a contemporary. These two young men collected a few Catalan dances and shortly afterwards collaborated on an orchestral suite using these called *Mont Juic* that appeared the following year. That work was to be dedicated 'In memory of Peter Burra'. Burra was a friend of Peter Pears, from Lancing College schooldays, with both literary and musical interests, and in 1936 he too was in Barcelona, writing reviews for *The Times*. From Spain, he wrote to Pears in London of his pleasure in Lennox Berkeley's company and also that of the young Britten – 'he's a *good* person'. Burra and Pears shared a maisonette in Charlotte Street, London, and after the Barcelona meeting with Burra Britten visited them there once or twice in early 1937. Then, in April 1937, Burra went flying with a friend in a two-seater private plane, with the idea of getting an aerial view of a cottage near Newbury which he had been lent and in which he was working on some writing; the aircraft crashed and although the pilot survived Peter Burra was killed. The sad but necessary task of going through his papers fell to Peter Pears. Britten had also recently been bereaved – his mother had died in January – and he went round to Charlotte Street to help. A relationship between the two men began, and it deepened into intimacy: it was to last almost exactly forty years, until the composer's death in December 1976.

A relationship of an altogether different kind is described in a Britten diary entry for 28 July 1937. 'Hair cut –' he writes,

> & then lunch with William Walton at Sloane Square. He is charming, but I feel always the school relationship with him – he is so obviously the head-prefect of English music, whereas I'm the promising young new boy. Soon of course he'll leave & return as a member of the staff – [Vaughan] Williams being of course the Headmaster. Elgar was never *that* – but a member of the Governing Board. Anyhow apart from a few slight reprimands (as to musical opinions) I am patronised in a very friendly manner. Perhaps the prefect is already regretting the lost freedom, & newly found authority!

At this time also the composer was thinking about a change

of residence. His sister Beth, with whom he had shared a Finchley Road flat for two years, was making her own life and in fact she married in January 1938. Britten now spent much of his time with Peter Pears in Charlotte Street, from where the singer walked each morning to take part in the broadcast Morning Service from Broadcasting House in Langham Place. But Britten was shortly to acquire a place of his own. On his mother's death he inherited £1000 and with this sum he purchased, in October 1937, a house in Suffolk, the Old Mill at Snape near Aldeburgh. Whatever the attractions of London, and indeed its convenience for a freelance composer, the county and countryside of his birth still drew him. He gave up his four-day-a-week salaried post with the GPO Film Unit and moved down to Snape in April 1938.

1937 had been a fruitful year for composition. There was, in February, incidental music for the Auden-Isherwood play *The Ascent of F6* whose director Rupert Doone found him 'pale, boyish, indefatigable.' The first night at the Mercury Theatre was something of a triumph and in a diary entry, a cheerful composer described the after-show party – 'I play & play & play, while the whole cast dances & sings & fools'. Critical reception was mixed, however, and the *Spectator* reviewer Derek Verschoyle thought that 'the incidental music composed by Mr Benjamin Britten was both unnecessary and unpleasing'. Other incidental music commissions kept him busy: a play by Louis MacNeice at the Westminster Theatre, two GPO films, a feature film called *Love from a Stranger*, and two BBC features also. The *Variations on a Theme of Frank Bridge* for string orchestra were commissioned by the conductor Boyd Neel for a Salzburg Festival concert and sketched out in ten intensively creative days in early June. Peter Pears (but not Britten himself) attended the Salzburg concert on 27 August, where, as Boyd Neel tells us, the work 'caused a major sensation'; it earned itself fifty further performances over the next couple of years, both in Europe and America. A song cycle with piano called *On This Island* to Auden's words, dates from October 1937 and received its première in a broadcast on 19 November by Sophie Wyss and the composer. Dedicated to Christopher Isherwood, the cycle seems something of a response to the Auden circle and its ideas; it was also Britten's first attempt at contemporary poetry. The sheer cleverness of Auden's verse half-conceals its sensuality – 'And the active hands must freeze/Lonely, on the sep'rate knees', for example – but Britten's music responds with naked intensity, as in the last couplet of the first song, 'And my vows break/Before his look'. Auden was later to describe Britten's sensitivity to words as 'extraordinary'. It dated, as we have seen, from his childhood and his extensive reading of both prose and poetry. Before the official première of *On This Island*, Britten had heard the songs sung by Peter Pears. Pears was not yet known as a solo singer – otherwise, doubtless, the first performance would have been entrusted to him – but on 15 October he sang the new songs for Lennox Berkeley and Christopher Isherwood. In his diary Britten wrote: 'Peter sings them well – if he studies he will be a very good singer. He's certainly one of the nicest people I know, but frightfully reticent.' Years later, as Pears remembers, Britten was to re-read, and be amused by, that forgotten diary entry.

Britten's 'socialistic inclinations', as he himself described a viewpoint that was really humanitarian rather than doctrinaire, were at their strongest in this period, that is from about 1936 to 1939. To a schoolboy's idealistic pacifism, encouraged by Frank Bridge, had been added the quasi-Marxist sympathies of Auden and his friends, indeed of many English intellectuals in the thirties. Britten's diaries show him as profoundly disturbed by the events in Abyssinia and Spain. When Auden went off to the Spanish Civil War in January 1937 Britten was 'terribly sad & I feel ghastly about it, tho' I feel it is perhaps the logical thing for him to do ... phenomenally brave'. (In fact the poet was back in early March, not very gloriously, having been refused permission by the Republican Government to drive an ambulance – perhaps they knew about his driving ability!) Britten himself felt, as Donald Mitchell has put it, 'that the artist's duty was to go on creating, not to participate in destruction, and instead to attempt to influence and persuade and modify'. (Later he was to declare 'I disbelieve profoundly in power and violence.') In the meantime he agreed in April 1937 to adopt a Spanish evacuee boy; but this plan came to nothing.

Away from London, things were more peaceful. The Old Mill

at Snape was in the reassuring Suffolk countryside of Britten's boyhood. He was not yet restless like Auden, not yet as ready to uproot himself from England and bid farewell 'to the house with its wallpaper red/. . . The works for two pianos' - though Auden's inscription of these words on the flyleaf of Britten's Sinfonietta score was a hint that he should be. He liked his Old Mill, wigwam-like in shape and converted into a dwelling-house in 1934. He had a radiogram there, a house-warming present from his publisher Ralph Hawkes, that received 'any station from Omsk to Tomsk - even the London Regional which is such a problem on the East Coast'. Peter Pears often travelled down to Suffolk, and so did other friends: Montagu Slater came with his wife Enid, who snapped a happily relaxed Britten playing pub darts, and Lennox Berkeley arrived in a sporty AC car that Britten liked to drive fast through the local lanes. Another visitor was the American composer Aaron Copland, invited for a summer weekend in 1938 following on a chance meeting with Britten in London; as well as playing each other their recent music they spent a day sunbathing on the beach with Britten's friends and local relatives. Copland was without a publisher at this time, and Britten found time to write to Ralph Hawkes recommending him - 'I feel he's a winner somehow'. He trusted his publisher, and was grateful to him, and once wrote to Hawkes, who had sent him a Verdi score: 'It isn't only for *Rigoletto* that I want to thank you - trying not to be sloppy - it is for all you've done for me, as Sponsor, Publisher, Agent, Maecenas - what you will. I don't think any composer starting out could have met with such luck as I have.'

In the summer of 1938 Britten completed a big new Piano Concerto, which he dedicated to Lennox Berkeley. He had played it to Copland, who had been struck by its pianistic flair but had reservations 'as to the substance of the musical materials'. Britten himself was the soloist on the occasion of its first performance: for a fee of eight guineas he played it on 18 August at a Promenade Concert in London with the BBC Symphony Orchestra conducted by Sir Henry Wood. In a programme note he called it 'a bravura Concerto . . . simple and direct in form' but described the goose-stepping march finale as having 'a somewhat jingoistic dialogue . . . a feeling of doubt creeps into the music ... the mood becomes more and more tense ... (finally) the orchestra shouts the march in all its swagger ... and the music rushes headlong to its confident finish.'

The reception of the Piano Concerto was mixed. The *Musical Times* critic, William McNaught, may or may not have read the programme note; but at any rate he disliked the emotional tone of the music. 'Mr Britten's cleverness, of which he has frequently been told,' he declared, 'has got the better of him and led him into all sorts of errors, the worst of which are errors of taste.' In fact the march finale of the Concerto may be related to other Britten marches of the thirties: wholly un-Elgarian pieces, tight-lipped and often bitter as doubtless befits a pacifist composer. This family of characteristic Britten marches includes the second of the *Frank Bridge Variations*, the march in the unfinished 'Go play, boy, play' string quartet (later transformed into 'Parade' in *Les Illuminations*), that of the violin and piano Suite, and the musically quite undistinguished *Pacifist March* of 1937. (In 1945 Britten was to revise the Piano Concerto; the third of its four movements was discarded and a new one substituted. Sviatoslav Richter's 1970 recording, under the composer's direction, has done something to rehabilitate a work that has never been especially popular.)

The winter of 1938–39 saw a steady darkening of the European political scene. Britten's composing went on apace, but he produced no 'concert' music as such, preferring to work in the film studio or theatre and for preference, at such a time, on political subjects. There was a choral piece called *Advance Democracy*. More important and substantial was the *Ballad of Heroes* for voices and orchestra that was first performed at a festival of 'Music for the People' on 5 April 1939. The text was by Auden and the journalist Randall Swingler, and the whole work was intended as an *in memoriam* piece for members of the British battalion of the International Brigade who had died in the Spanish Civil War. Its four movements incorporated a Funeral March and a scherzo 'Dance of Death' – exactly as *Our Hunting Fathers* had done three years earlier – and in the scherzo Britten used verses from the Auden 'farewell' poem of lament for a dying Europe ('It's farewell to the drawing-room's civilised cry') that he had now known for a couple of years.

By this time Auden had already gone: on 18 January 1939 he and Christopher Isherwood had taken a boat train from Waterloo *en route* for the United States. 'I never wish to see England again,' he wrote to a friend. Britten was in general agreement with Auden's view that artists now working in England felt 'essentially lonely, twisted in dying roots'. Furthermore, English musical opinion grudged its praise for his work. For example, Constant Lambert – himself a composer and also the conductor of the *Ballad for Heroes* première – had written of him: 'Mr Britten is, I admit, rather a problem to me. One cannot but admire his extremely mature and economical methods, yet the rather drab and penitential content of his music leaves me quite unmoved. At the same time he is the most outstanding talent of his generation and I would always go to hear any first performance of his.' Like William McNaught, whose view of the Piano Concerto is quoted above, Lambert recognised Britten's gifts but simply disliked the emotional tone of his music. Perhaps this is understandable. The music was disturbing and, as Peter Pears has said, 'the English do not like brilliance, particularly in the young.'

Finally the composer made his decision, and in May 1939 Britten and Pears followed the Auden-Isherwood example and sailed for the United States, or more precisely for Canada and then shortly afterwards New York. Sensibly, there were positive as well as negative reasons for the journey: forthcoming performances of Britten's music in America, and also the possibility of a Hollywood film commission, though in fact this came to nothing. In December 1979, Peter Pears told me: 'Why we went to America, really, was partly of course the sort of problem – the dilemma – in front of one. Was one going to stay and be a pacifist, and face that? Or was one going to offer oneself to Friends' Relief, or whatever it might be, doing the sort of helpful things one could do? There seemed no point. Ben was browned off about things; and I had left the BBC, and there wasn't very much outlook for me either. He had, I think, a definite offer, which later fell through, of a film in Hollywood about King Arthur. When we arrived in America we still thought that he was going to have a film. But it must have been clear quite soon that it wasn't so.'

One wonders to what extent Britten himself thought of the departure for America as a turning point in his career. He could look back over twenty compositions, some substantial, and as many scores of incidental music for the cinema, theatre and radio. He had a publisher's contract, and that ensured that all his music received performance; Boosey & Hawkes had their offices not only in London, but also in Sydney, Cape Town, Paris, Toronto and New York – indeed it was partly for that reason that he and Pears were visiting Toronto before travelling to New York, where a performance of his *Frank Bridge Variations* awaited him on 21 August. The New York Philharmonic Orchestra were to play this work, and it was undoubtedly through the influence of his publisher that this performance was taking place. Britten had some reason to be optimistic about his future as a composer in America. Possibly, too, his musical style would find a readier response than it had done in England. In the event, he was to be disappointed.

4

America (1939–41)

Dé - part dans l'af-fec - tion   et   le bruit neufs.

Les Illuminations

Though the Atlantic crossing of early 1939 was Britten's first, Peter Pears had already visited the United States on two occasions with the New English Singers, and their friends Auden and Isherwood were established in a New York apartment. Britten was of course going not as a tourist but as a working musician, with at least the possibility of eventually taking up American citizenship, and Pears's situation was similar. The terms of the standard entry visa forbade the taking of paid employment, however, and Auden had got into trouble over this very point and been obliged to leave the country and re-enter it as a 'legal British immigrant' from Canada before he could work. Britten and Pears avoided this problem. They sailed first to Quebec Province for a holiday, and then went to Toronto, from where after a few weeks they could quite legally travel to New York, free to work there as opportunity offered. On the train Britten wrote to a friend, characteristically summing up his immediate past, present feelings and future prospects.

I'm writing now as I don't know when I shall have a moment again, they keep us on the run so. We had a terrific time in Toronto & really met some charming people. They seemed to

like having a real live composer round about, & made, what
seemed to me, a ridiculous fuss! Interviews were priceless –
I'll let you see some sometime! Had two Radio shows – & I've
been asked to write a special work for the CBC at Toronto
and play it myself in August. I'm looking forward to New
York. But also feeling a bit nervous about it – with all its
sophistication & 'New Yorker' brightness. I can't do that sort
of thing very well. However, I hope we'll find a nice place
to settle down in for a bit – near Cape Cod or Boston – I
want to do some more work.

The 'nice place to settle down in' was to be found with Pears's
friends the Mayer family, who lived at Amityville on Long
Island. Pears had crossed the Atlantic with the New English
Singers in 1936 and Mrs Elizabeth Mayer (to whom he had an
introduction from a friend) was on the same boat. They had
made friends: she was, he found, 'the very best kind of German',
a woman of warmth and intelligence who was leaving Hitler's
Europe for New York, where her husband, a neurologist, was to
join her later. By the time Britten and Pears arrived in New
York in late June, 1939 the Mayer family were living at Stanton
Cottage, in the grounds of a Long Island home for mentally
disturbed patients of which Dr William Mayer was medical
director. From the George Washington Hotel Pears wrote to
Mrs Mayer: 'I and my friend Benjamin Britten, composer, have
just arrived in New York, and I am so looking forward to seeing
you again.' Pears invited Mrs Mayer to lunch with them and
the friendship was quickly renewed. Elizabeth Mayer was a
highly artistic person, indeed a former music student, and she
took to Britten at once. A couple of months later, after the two
young musicians had travelled about a little, they returned to
New York for the performance of the *Frank Bridge Variations*
on 21 August, spending that weekend at the Mayers' home. It
was the longest 'weekend' of their lives, lasting, on and off, until
their return to England in March 1942.

At twenty-five, Britten had lost both his parents; now, in New
York, he seemed far from the physical and psychological landscape of his happy childhood. In the warmth of the Mayer
household he was delighted once again to feel part of a family.

There were William and Elizabeth Mayer, their daughter Beata and son Christopher; an older son, Michael, was in the US Army and a younger daughter, Ulrika, was also not always at home. The house was fairly small and when everyone was there it bulged at the seams; but whoever might have to sleep in a camp bed on the porch, it was unlikely to be the young composer, who had his own domain complete with piano. Elizabeth Mayer 'was mad about Ben', Pears recalls: she loved him indeed as another son.

Yet despite the family warmth and kindness, Britten was at this time 'muddled, fed-up, discouraged' – his own words. He was often dissatisfied with the music he wrote. Besides this, he was now also finding it hard to earn a living. The music-loving owner of a local hardware store, David Rothman, set up a concert for Britten and Pears, and when virtually no audience turned up Britten, in tears, talked rather wildly of working at the Rothman store instead of spending all his time on music. David Rothman tried vainly to reassure him: 'I told him, keep going. Look, you're only about twenty-six years old. You've already done well, because Koussevitzky and the Boston Symphony have performed your work. They did a Violin Concerto with the New York Philharmonic. What do you want, blood?' Beata Mayer remembers a time when Britten was 'in the blackest of moods ... he had a sort of block. And Mother suggested he go out to Jones Beach, long road along the sea, miles and miles, and it was in winter and it was perfectly empty. And he drove like mad – she never forgot it, she was so scared – he drove at enormous speed, for hours, up and down that long, long stretch along the beach. And they went home, and the next morning Mother came and said, "he is writing again".'

Such bouts of gloom and restlessness recurred throughout Britten's time in the United States. It was not the common depression of a composer who has written music that he then cannot get performed. Indeed on paper, Britten's career was successful: new works were written and they received performances, thanks no doubt to the efficiency of Boosey & Hawkes whose support for their young composer never wavered.

And these new pieces were in most cases of major importance. Admittedly *Young Apollo*, a piece for piano and string orchestra commissioned by the Canadian Broadcasting Corporation and played by the composer in Toronto in August 1939, dissatisfied him and he left it unpublished. But the substantial and beautiful Violin Concerto, completed on 20 September and mainly written at St Jovite in the province of Quebec, shows a clear mastery; totally different from the Piano Concerto of the previous year, it has an elegiac quality despite the virtuoso writing for the soloist. Its first interpreter, the Spaniard Antonio Brosa, was to see Spanish elements in the work – perhaps a sadness for the Spain Britten had visited and then seen torn by its civil war. When Brosa came in 1940 to America, where he was to settle during the war years, Britten entrusted the Violin Concerto to him and he gave its first performance with the New York Philharmonic Orchestra under John Barbirolli on 28 March 1940. A song cycle with string orchestra, to texts from Rimbaud's *Les Illuminations*, had received a partial performance (the songs 'Being Beauteous' and 'Marine' at a London Promenade Concert on 17 August 1939, with Sophie Wyss) and then was completed at Amityville on 25 October; Sophie Wyss gave it the following January in London with the Boyd Neel Orchestra, and in the following May Peter Pears sang it in New York as part of the International Society for Contemporary Music Festival held there. *Les Illuminations* is a work of exceptionally strong personality, yet at the same time it possesses a subtlety that was new in Britten; and while the virtuoso brilliance of 'Villes' or 'Parade' evokes the intoxication of a crowded city at night, the cycle ends with the intense quiet sadness of 'Départ' – '*Assez vu . . . Assez eu . . . Assez connu . . . Départ dans l'affection et le bruit neufs*' (Enough seen, had, known . . . departure towards new loves, new sounds)'. A more extrovert piece, the *Canadian Carnival* for orchestra, received a BBC broadcast from Bristol in June 1940, though it was not heard in concert performance until Britten himself conducted it in England five years later, at Cheltenham on 12 June 1945, just five days after the première of *Peter Grimes*.

Britten's first 'symphony', if we exclude the *Simple Symphony* for strings, was the *Sinfonia da Requiem*. This was written in 1940 as a commissioned work: the British Council had approached him for a symphony for a foreign festival that proved to be a dynastic celebration in Japan. Though the Japanese authorities initially approved the composer's scheme for a 'requiem symphony' with its attendant Christian overtones, after the completed score was handed over Britten received a furious protest via the Japanese Embassy stating that the work represented an insult to the Mikado and must be rejected. With Auden's help Britten wrote a reply; but in any case communications were soon severed following upon the Japanese attack on Pearl Harbor. The *Sinfonia da Requiem* is short – a mere twenty minutes – but intensely dramatic, its three movements being headed with the titles 'Lacrymosa', 'Dies irae' and 'Requiem aeternam'. All three, unusually, share the same key, D – for 'death', perhaps? – but while the central scherzo is a characteristic Britten 'dance of death' piece, the finale, after rising to a broad climax, dies away in a mood of gentle benediction. (The closing pages of the *War Requiem* a decade later have the same key centre and are similar in mood.) The première of the *Sinfonia da Requiem* took place on 30 March 1941; Barbirolli conducted the New York Philharmonic Orchestra.

Two other commissioned works were the *Diversions* for piano (left hand) and orchestra and the First String Quartet. The *Diversions* were composed for the one-armed Austrian pianist Paul Wittgenstein (who had also had music written for him by Ravel and Prokofiev) and he gave their first performance with the Philadelphia Orchestra under Eugene Ormandy on 16 January 1942. The Quartet was a commission from the well-known patroness of music, Mrs Elizabeth Sprague Coolidge, a lady who possessed musical gifts and judgement as well as the means to encourage musicians. This four-movement work was written in July 1941 and first performed by the Coolidge String Quartet in September in Los Angeles. With this work Britten won a Library of Congress Medal for Services to Chamber Music.

All this hardly constitutes a record of failure. What then does Peter Pears mean when he says that during this American period 'things seemed to be going from bad to worse' for Britten and himself? Partly, the problems were financial. Despite the performance royalties that came Britten's way, he and Pears were in no position to establish a home of their own. They were unhappy about the darkening scene that they had left behind, with their friends and families in wartime Europe. But from

Britten's point of view what was deeply worrying also was the mainly adverse criticism that greeted his music in America. Pears puts it bluntly: 'He had terrible reviews.' And Beata Mayer has amplified this theme: 'He was terribly sensitive to criticism . . . and he got lots of bad reviews in America – I mean, Americans didn't like him. They really crushed him.'

In this psychological climate it was not wholly surprising that Britten's health started to break down. At Amityville he suffered much from throat trouble, culminating in a streptoccocal infection in 1940 during which Beata Mayer literally nursed him back from the brink of death. Auden, characteristically, thought this illness psychosomatic, an expression of uncertainty of purpose. (A future friend, William Plomer, was to make the same point, suggesting that disease was a kind of protest of the individual against his environment, and that 'when this protest is against not only his life but the way that the world is ordered, then the disease is deep-seated indeed.') All that his friends could do, in the meantime, was to remind him that other artists had passed through despair, and that so long as he went on *experiencing* he would continue to compose – which, for him, was synonymous with being alive.

Britten's serious illness in 1940 was, as it were, merely a peak of sickness in a life that was never quite free of health troubles. At the age of three months, he had had pneumonia quite seriously, and his mother had to feed him with breast milk from a fountain-pen filler. Though he recovered, he never became altogether strong as a boy, and there were suggestions of a heart murmur for which various tests were carried out. At the Royal College in London he seems to have kept reasonably well, but in America, as Beata Mayer recalls: 'He was constantly ill. I mean, he had sore throats and sometimes got very ill too. And I had been a nurse in Italy, where I lived for four years, but whenever Ben was sick I was called upon to look after him even one time, when they were in Maine, I was called to come up there. He always was frail: he got this terrible throat infection. And Mother worried about him.'

Thus, the received impression of Britten as a wiry, athletic composer who liked to swim, play tennis and exercise his dog, while not inaccurate, remains only a part of the truth. For just as in his music he seems to have felt the need to overcome self-set challenges, so he seems also to have defied chronic ill-health. There was always a counterpoint in him, too, between the themes of physical/psychological health and executant/creative music. In later life he could not eat, and then keep down, food before playing in a concert, for the tension he felt had a powerful physical effect. In his opera *Death in Venice* he was deliberately to equate physical disease with moral unease; and in a curious way, perhaps, physical sickness, and moral ambiguity too, provided a fertile soil in which his art could flourish. As Aschenbach, obsessed by the young boy Tadzio, soliloquises towards the end of *Death in Venice*: 'What is reason, moral sense, what is art itself, compared to the rewards of chaos? ... Chaos and sickness... What if all were dead and only we two left alive?'

It was of course not only to Beata Mayer that Britten owed his recovery from illness. There was also the devoted care, and love, of Peter Pears. Now, in 1940, he composed a set of songs especially for his friend. These were settings of sonnets by Michelangelo, and there was significance in the choice of these seven texts, love poems addressed to a young man both handsome in person and noble in character. As for the dedication, 'to Peter', this was the first time he had used a simple Christian name in this way. (The only previous song dedicated to Pears, as 'P.N.L.P.', is 'Being Beauteous' in *Les Illuminations*, the only love song incidentally in that cycle.) The comparison with *Les Illuminations* is instructive. The boy poet of *Les Illuminations*, Rimbaud, had been impulsive and even Dionysiac; the mature artist Michelangelo offered texts in which an intense personal feeling was disciplined, Apollonian, and heroic. Here was an expression of love that was both strong and noble.

In 1979 Pears recalled the inception of the *Michelangelo Sonnets* as follows: 'We did quite a number of concerts in aid of British War Relief. And for that programme we usually did some English songs to start with, generally Purcell, and then a group of Schubert, and then after the interval some songs by Ben. And he wanted to write a cycle for us, which was in fact the first cycle he'd written for me; and he pitched on the Michelangelo sonnets. Now this was partly I think because he wanted to get away from the sort of poem which was being set, and had been set, in

England over quite a long period: that is, either the Housman or the Elizabethans. He really wanted to try his wings a bit further than that; and we decided – I think *he* really decided – on the Michelangelo. He had set *Les Illuminations*, the Rimbaud earlier, a year or so before and had enjoyed it very much, it had worked very well, and he still thought he would take another trip abroad before he returned to the English poets. And we went through the Michelangelo sonnets together; our Italian was not very expert, but we had a translation on the other side of the page and used to read them through and see how they sounded – and what matched, in what order they should come and so on – and finally he finished them. We didn't do a public performance in the States at that time – we only did a private performance there. But when we got back to England in '42 we began to work at them, and we gave the first performance in fact in the autumn at the Wigmore Hall. They were warmly received and were clearly something new and brilliant and touching. They were the first of a whole row of works which he wrote for me. Needless to say, it was for me a tremendous occasion and one that I very deeply appreciated. They have indeed on that account – as well as others – a very special meaning for me.'

The *Michelangelo Sonnets* were completed at the Mayers' on 30 October 1940. By then Britten and Pears had lived for over a year at Stanton Cottage. During all this time they had been much more than house guests, and their friends had become the Mayers' also: thus Auden was at Britten's birthday party on 22 November 1939 and became a frequent visitor. Yet perhaps they felt they were imposing on their hosts and should become more independent. When Auden moved into a Brooklyn house in which most of the rooms were rented by artists, Pears and Britten decided to join him in what was in effect an artistic colony, moving there in November 1940.

Their new home at 7 Middagh Street, Brooklyn Heights, offered a life style which was the closest that Britten ever got to 'liberated', not to say Bohemian living. It was an experiment that was in some ways valuable, but that he had no wish to repeat. He and Pears occupied a large room on the top floor; Wystan Auden, and later his American boy friend, Chester

Kallman, were on that same floor. The house was rented by George Davis of *Harper's Bazaar* magazine, and its other tenants included the stripper (and author) Gypsy Rose Lee, Carson McCullers and Paul Bowles (both writers) and Bowles's wife Jane, together with Thomas Mann's son Golo. Later short-term lodgers were Louis MacNeice and Salvador and Gala Dali. All the visitors had to be approved by Auden and they were without exception strong artistic and/or social personalities; one visitor, Denis de Rougemont, went so far as to say that 'all that was new in America in music, painting or choreography emanated from that house, the only center of thought and art that I found in any large city of the country'. The daytime routine was of work and good hot regular meals with Auden at the head of the table keeping order; as for Britten, he could work on a Steinway piano in a first-floor 'parlor' room. In the evening the atmosphere relaxed: there were gay parties (in both senses of the word) and plenty to drink. Even so, neither Britten nor Pears were totally at ease at Middagh Street; Auden, too, may have resented his former quasi-disciple's relationship with Pears, in which he rightly recognised the diminution of his own influence. Nevertheless the period at 7 Middagh Street saw the creation of the biggest single work produced by Britten and Auden in collaboration: this was the operetta *Paul Bunyan*. But in the summer of 1941 Britten and Pears left Middagh Street for California. When they returned to New York it was once again to the Mayers' at Amityville that they went.

Over something like a decade, Britten had been ranging more and more widely stylistically, and indeed (as it were) geographically. Alongside the clearly 'English' works like *A Boy was Born* and the 'Holiday Diary', there had been the *Quatre chansons françaises* and the somewhat 'central-European' Sinfonietta. The Rossini arrangements of his *Soirées Musicales* in 1936 had taken him to Italy, while the *Frank Bridge Variations* (with their individual titles in four languages) had been something of a European tour; *Mont Juic* had used Catalan dances and the Violin Concerto also had a Spanish flavour, at least in the view of its first interpreter Antonio Brosa. There were clear Russian features in the two concertos – Britten knew his Prokofiev and Shostakovich – and also of course in the piece called *Russian*

Funeral for brass and percussion that dates from 1936. *Les Illuminations* was again 'French' and the *Michelangelo Sonnets* Renaissance-Italian. As for the *Sinfonia da Requiem*, it was European in the broadest sense, a work of the western Christian tradition.

The last three of these works were all completed after Britten crossed the Atlantic. Clearly his departure from Europe had by no means destroyed his artistic roots there. Where, we may wonder, was the new 'American' style that might have been expected of an artist so demonstrably adaptable, so magpie-like in his fruitful grasping of different idioms? In point of fact, American indigenous music had made some mark on his work even before he left Europe in 1939: there are blues in the *Ascent of F6* incidental music (used again in some *Cabaret Songs*) and the Piano Concerto (whose blues section was to disappear in later revision), while the last song of *On This Island* ('As it is, plenty') is a pert ragtime number.

And yet the New World had so far yielded only something limited in musical resources. His friend Aaron Copland had identified the problem, which indeed was still more acute for an American-born composer. Though jazz was an obvious native idiom, it was restricting: 'it was an easy way to be American in musical terms, but all American music could not possibly be confined to two dominant jazz moods, the blues and the snappy number'. Copland's ideal in the 1920s, after he returned from study under Nadia Boulanger in Paris, was to write music 'that would immediately be recognised as American in character ... that could speak of universal things in a vernacular of American speech rhythms ... that left popular music far behind – music with a largeness of utterance'. He achieved his aim by going back beyond urban jazz and swing idioms to real country music, to cowboy songs in *Billy the Kid*, pious Shaker songs in *Appalachian Spring*, and dances like the waltz and hoedown in *Rodeo*. He may have sowed these seeds of a broader American musical style when he visited Britten at Snape in 1938 and played him his new 'school opera', *The Second Hurricane*. This was music of the great outdoors, of a new country created by vision as well as labour. Its mood of simplicity and vigour, of innocence even, was exactly the key to inspire Britten to create his own 'American style'. The eventual fruit of this inspiration was *Paul Bunyan* in 1941.

Boosey & Hawkes, Britten's publishers, had suggested that he and Wystan Auden should devise a theatrical piece for American high schools. The idea was attractive to both men: they liked young people with their unspoilt freshness and enthusiasm, while Britten at least still believed in the 'civilising' and educative power of art. The project went ahead, and in a few months of 1940–41 they wrote a substantial two-act 'operetta' for production in May 1941 at Columbia University in New York.

In a programme note, the two collaborators explained their story and its intention. Paul Bunyan tells the pioneer myth of a giant lumberman who tames the virgin forests of America so that civilisation may take root there, and he is

> a projection of the collective state of mind of a people whose tasks were primarily the physical mastery of nature. This operetta presents in a compressed fairy-story form the development of the continent from a virgin forest before the birth of Paul Bunyan to settlement and cultivation when Paul Bunyan says goodbye because he is no longer needed, i.e. the human task is now a different one, of how to live well in a country that the pioneers have made it possible to live in.

Elsewhere Auden explained that although it might seem presumptuous for two Englishmen to deal with this American tale, the implications of the story were universal.

Paul Bunyan demonstrates fully what Copland has called Britten's 'wonderful naturalness' in its characteristically sure grasp of an American musical vernacular which was ballad-like and in 'country style'. Britten also used a 'big number' choral-orchestral technique that he had gleaned from Broadway shows. The narrator's part was given to a ballad singer accompanied on stage by guitar and bass, a kind of country band in fact, whose music is both simple and right. Britten did not forget that *Paul Bunyan* was a work for high school youngsters, although as it happened the première was given by adults. But, of course, there is more to an opera than the music. The libretto provided by Auden seems much less well focused stylistically. Indeed one must consider its literary virtuosity wholly misapplied. Not only were there lines like 'Appendectomy/'s a pain in the neck to me', there were self-indulgent and unintelligible references to Cézanne, Peer Gynt, St Sebastian the Martyr and the Yiddish Alps. Auden must have known, too, that in New York the line 'A fairy stood beside his bed' would get the wrong kind of laughs. He was doubtless right when, twenty years later, he blamed himself for *Paul Bunyan*'s failure: 'I was entirely to blame, since, at the time, I knew nothing whatever about opera or what is required of a librettist. In consequence, some very lovely music of Britten's went down the drain, and I must now belatedly make my apologies to my old friend.'

The New York critics disliked *Paul Bunyan*. Virgil Thomson, whose *Herald Tribune* review was headed 'Musico-Theatrical Flop', thought the music witty but otherwise without distinction. In *The New Yorker*, the work was called 'anemic, bewildering and irritating'. On the other hand, the audience received the operetta favourably and the cast enjoyed playing the work. Five years later, at the time of *Peter Grimes*, Britten was to write of *Bunyan*: 'The critics damned it unmercifully, but the public seemed to find something enjoyable in the performances. Despite the criticisms, I wanted to write more works for the stage.' But in the meantime, he was wounded by the failure. He withdrew *Paul Bunyan* from the list of his works. (Only in 1974–75 after Auden's death and not long before his own, did he revise it and permit its revival.)

Paul Bunyan could have marked the beginning of an era. It was Britten's first wholly 'American' work: its pioneering mythical story seems now to represent the cultural roots he himself might have put down in America, while its purpose as a piece for high schools suggests a practical look forward to further work in school music. Its failure was a slap in the face from the American musical establishment. It also dealt a severe blow to Britten's friendship and collaboration with Auden. There was no sudden ending: Auden started work on a Christmas oratorio for Britten to set, though that came to nothing since Britten found the text unwieldy, and he also wrote the *Hymn to St Cecilia* for Britten as a kind of personal tribute. But that was the end of the collaboration, underlined by Britten's return to England in early 1942. Later, Britten was to consider *Our Hunting Fathers* their most successful joint venture.

Perhaps the return of Britten and Pears was determined, more or less, by the reception of *Paul Bunyan*. The two musicians were still, after two years, hesitating to take up American citizenship; and though they may even have acquired the necessary forms, these remained uncompleted. What Donald Mitchell has called a 'tidal pull' seems to have exerted its pressure. The metaphor is apt, for the force drawing Britten back to England was, despite its strength, at first hardly to be felt. After *Bunyan* he and Pears went in the opposite direction, to the West Coast, staying with Ethel and Rae Robertson and writing two-piano music for them as well as the *Scottish Ballad* for two pianos and orchestra and his First String Quartet. (At least, it was his first *published* string quartet: but there had been another, written ten years before as a student work for Frank Bridge, and perhaps he was reminded of England and of his old teacher, who had recently died.) He wrote to an English friend confessing that he found in America 'the faults of Europe without the attractiveness. The present chauvinism in their arts is horrifying – & most of their art is pretty lousy. But as soon as the war is over I'm coming back.'

But, of course, Britten and Pears returned much sooner than that. The story of their discovery of Crabbe's poetry and the Peter Grimes story has already been told in Chapter 1. As Pears recalls, it induced 'a tremendous nostalgia in Ben and we then and there decided that we must go home, and ... we almost immediately started to apply for a passage home, which was not at all easy to get in those days.' Back with the Mayers in New York, Britten wrote to Mrs Elizabeth Sprague Coolidge:

> I have made up my mind to return to England, at any rate for the duration of the war. I am not telling people, because it sounds a little heroic, which it is far from being; it is really that I cannot be separated any longer from all my friends and family–going through all they are–and I'm afraid will be in the future. I think I shall be able to continue with my work over there, which is what I most want to do, of course. I don't actually know when I shall be sailing, since boats are so scarce & heavily booked up – and anyhow I have so much to get

finished here, so I may not be leaving much before Christmas. But please be back before I go!

Even now, as we see, Britten was hesitating – or pretending, to himself as well as others, to hesitate. Not about the return to England, which was now decided, but about its irreversibility. Consciously, too, he identified the need to return in terms of his friends and family; but unconsciously perhaps it was the whole world of his childhood that drew him. His future was uncertain, and as wartime pacifists he and Pears faced prejudice and animosity, possibly even imprisonment if they were not granted exemption from military service. But as so often with him, tension and worry accelerated the creative process. By the time he and Pears reached England in April 1942 Britten had written the *Hymn to St Cecilia* and *A Ceremony of Carols* – both highly 'English' pieces – and, together with Pears, sketched out a synopsis of the opera set in his native Suffolk, *Peter Grimes*.

5

In wartime England
(1942–45)

Allegro molto

PETER (p)

I am na- tive,— root- ed here.—

Peter Grimes, Act I

'I may not be leaving much before Christmas,' Britten had written in the late summer of 1941 from New York. It was not until 16 March 1942 that he finally wrote in the Mayers' visitors' book, 'The end of the weekend', in affectionate reference to their first entry in August 1939. Having at last secured a passage to England, he and Peter Pears embarked on the Swedish cargo ship *Axel Johnson*, which after various stops up the coast finally set out from the Canadian port of Halifax.

The Atlantic crossing, in that third year of the war, was long (the voyage lasted four weeks), uncomfortable and hazardous. Britten was to have customs problems, not only in New York but on arriving in England also, over the manuscript music scores that he carried, which officialdom regarded with suspicion as possibly encoded material. His sister Beth remembers his account of the voyage: 'They were coming over in convoy, and it was in the days of the very bad submarine attacks in the North Atlantic, and in the middle of the Atlantic their funnel caught fire. And of course the convoy had to go on – they could wait for nobody. So there they were, a sitting target ... with a blazing funnel.' Peter Pears remembers the accommodation, 'a two-berth cabin which happened to be just opposite the large door of the ship's refrigerator . . . this used to be occasionally opened, and out would come a really appalling mixture of smells, which was not at all helpful to anyone suffering rather from sea-sickness. However, we survived.'

In the midst of all this, as we have seen, Britten went ahead with his composing. The New York customs had impounded (though only temporarily) a manuscript score of his unaccompanied vocal *Hymn to St Cecilia*, as yet not quite finished; he wrote it out again (having doubtless retained some sketches) and finished it on 2 April, dedicating it to Mrs Mayer. There were also some settings of early English (and Scottish) poems for treble voices and harp, to which he gave the unusual title, *A Ceremony of Carols*: they are preceded and followed by a plainchant procession and recession, and at one point the vocal sequence is broken by a truly angelic harp interlude (added later, as was the carol *That yongë child*). He and Pears also sketched a synopsis for *Peter Grimes*. Clearly his musical mind was now directed towards England and things English, just as his physical self was travelling 'home'. Over the next three years, until the Second String Quartet of 1945, all but one of his works (the Prelude and Fugue for string orchestra) were to be vocal, and to English words. Furthermore, they were mainly non-contemporary texts. The young composer, approaching thirty, had made his 'grand tour': at least for the time being, like Rimbaud, he had *assez vu*, and he wanted to put his roots down once again, not just in England but specifically in his native Suffolk.

When Britten and Pears arrived finally in the United Kingdom on 17 April 1942, they went first to London and then to East Anglia. Britten still owned the Old Mill at Snape: significantly, he had never made up his mind to sell this Suffolk property. However, in the meantime it had served as a home for his sister Beth, now Mrs Kit Welford, and her children while Dr Welford was on war service; later Kit Welford was invalided out and rejoined her there. But Britten and Pears now used the Old Mill as their home too. It was a place to relax and think in; the two musicians could rehearse there, and of course Britten could compose uninterrupted. 'Coming back to Suffolk was just like beginning again,' Pears has said. After the bustle of America, Suffolk provided peace, and space, and time to reflect – paradoxically, since it was Britain that was closer to the war. However, there was little sign of the war at Snape – at least, nothing like the London blitz or the flying bombs and V2 rockets that later were directed at the capital, though naturally there were food shortages. In any case, relative austerity hardly bothered Britten, who liked the plain food of his childhood. He could walk through the Suffolk fields and marshlands, seeing little traffic, breathing the air and listening to the cries of curlews and gulls, tranquilly absorbing an environment little changed since Crabbe's time. Sometimes he walked by the sea, where there were the 'expanses of mud, saltish commons, the marsh-birds crying'. It was the landscape of *Peter Grimes*, and the composer's mind was already moving towards the discovery and clarification of a musical language appropriate to his future opera.

When in London, Britten and Pears could stay with friends. One of these was Erwin Stein, the music editor at Boosey & Hawkes and a cultivated, sympathetic musician. But from 1943 they had their own flat at 45a St John's Wood High Street, in a by-no-means unattractive building (three storeys and an attic) with an antique shop occupying the ground floor; and they liked it enough to stay there for three years. Both had had a major hurdle to negotiate upon their return, an appearance before a tribunal to argue their pacifist case for exemption from military service. Fortunately this was granted, and they were free to pursue a musical career as a performing duo.

The two men had already been giving occasional recitals for some five years. Their first concerts were at Oxford and Cambridge during 1937, in aid of Spanish War relief organisations, and in America they had continued to perform as Pears steadily became a more established soloist, though they would still go together for lessons with his singing teacher Clytie Mundy. Now, from wartime London or Suffolk, they toured busily to various parts of Great Britain giving concerts under the auspices of the Council for the Encouragement of Music and the Arts (usually called simply CEMA). Imogen Holst has described their

wartime recitals in small towns and villages for a ram-shackle, poverty-stricken organisation which has since been transformed out of all recognition into the Arts Council of Great Britain. Their concerts were often fantastic adventures: they would have to find their way in the pouring rain down some dark, muddy East Anglian lane that was little better than a cart-track, until they eventually reached a desolate, tin-roofed village hall. Here they would find a smoking oil-stove in one corner and in the opposite corner an elderly upright piano with polished brass candle-brackets and panels of fretwork and faded pink silk. In the middle of the hall would be an audience of twenty or thirty people who had never been to a concert before, but who were enthralled by the singing and playing.

Of course Pears and Britten performed also in London and in other major cities. One concert-giving organisation in the capital, of particular interest since it existed only through the war years and just beyond, was the National Gallery Concerts, founded by the pianist Myra Hess, with chamber concerts held daily on weekdays during the lunch-hour in the National Gallery in Trafalgar Square. It was an inspired use for the building, which would otherwise have stood idle while its priceless collection of pictures was stored safely away, and the director, Kenneth Clark – who was later to become a good friend of Britten and Pears – and the trustees were glad to lend it. The concerts were usually crowded, with average audiences around six hundred; by 1943 half a million people had attended. (The 500,000th member of the audience arrived on 10 November 1943, a sailor home on leave.) Admission was always one shilling, and the artists' fees, whatever the performers' standing, were quite small. Some financial aid came from the United States and Canada, but usually the concerts made a profit; this went to a charity, the Musicians' Benevolent Fund. In all, the aim of the concerts was 'the threefold one of giving a large public cheap chamber concerts of the finest quality, employing a vast number of artists (many of them talented newcomers) hard hit during the war years, and offering substantial aid to an institution giving relief to needy, sick and aged musicians'.

Britten and Pears performed the *Seven Sonnets of Michelangelo*, preceded by Schumann's *Dichterliebe* song cycle at a National

Gallery concert on 22 October 1942. In fact this was the second performance of the *Sonnets* in London. They were first heard at the Wigmore Hall on 23 September 1942. This occasion was recalled in April 1980 by the *Daily Telegraph* critic Peter Stadlen. 'I vividly remember a crowded Wigmore Hall in September 1942, a mere five months after their return ... At the end, after a second or two of tense silence, a burst of tumultuous applause proved that music had won the day.' Presumably Stadlen means that there was some opposition to be overcome, perhaps from those who were disturbed or upset by the artists' conscientious objector status or by the homoerotic nature of Michelangelo's texts. But one might suppose that such people would hardly go out of their way to attend a Britten-Pears concert, save out of curiosity or malice. Whatever the climate of opinion (and there was undoubtedly some prejudice which lasted, though diminished, throughout Britten's life) it is worth redressing the balance and recalling that many people, professional musicians and otherwise, admired his gifts and were fond of him personally. His music had not been forgotten during his absence, and even the newer pieces from the American period had in some cases been heard – for example the Violin Concerto. As Peter Pears says, 'one of the astonishing things was the warmth of the reception of Ben back from America. In one or two small, not very important cases there were snaps and barks, but on the whole it was really extremely warm. The public was very warm.' He and Britten recorded the *Michelangelo Sonnets* for His Master's Voice in November 1942, this being the first of many recordings they were to make as a duo.

Possibly because he was busy concert-giving with Peter Pears, and perhaps also because he was writing radio documentary music, Britten produced no new concert works in the twelve months or so following upon his return to England in the spring of 1942. Still, there were the premières of the *Hymn to St Cecilia* (London, November 1942) and *A Ceremony of Carols* (Norwich, December 1942). Then in the early summer of 1943 he found himself prompted to make a musical gift to Boyd Neel and his orchestra, who had performed his *Frank Bridge Variations* so successfully in 1937 and who were now about to celebrate their 'tenth birthday' with a concert at the Wigmore Hall in London.

His Prelude and Fugue for Eighteen-part String Orchestra, which provided a solo for each player, was written for that occasion, 23 June 1943.

The year 1943 also brought a commission of significance for Britten's future work. This was a request for some church music; it came from the Rev. Walter Hussey and his church, St Matthew's in Northampton. Walter Hussey was an Anglican priest of strong artistic interests who regretted that the Christian church was no longer the kind of great patron of the arts that it had been for Michelangelo and Raphael – or in music, for Purcell, Bach, Haydn and even Liszt. The important composers of the late-nineteenth and early-twentieth century – or some at least, like Debussy, Sibelius, Schoenberg and Bartók – were scarcely associated with church music; and conversely, much of the music specially written for church use was of the second rank. Hussey had the enlightened notion of turning the forthcoming fiftieth anniversary of his church's consecration into an artistic as well as an ecclesiastical event. The celebration was to be in September 1943, and with a judgement that seems in retrospect singularly acute, Hussey approached artists who were young or relatively young, not yet 'grand old men' of the establishment whose services, in any case, his church could hardly afford: thus he went to the sculptor Henry Moore for a Madonna and Child and the painter Graham Sutherland for a crucifixion mural. These were men aged around forty, progressive and vital, yet of existing recognised achievement, One corresponding figure in English music was clearly William Walton, whose oratorio *Belshazzar's Feast* was imaginative and exciting; but an initial approach to Walton received first an equivocal and then a rather negative response. Time was passing, and with his good choir and organist (and a good four-manual instrument too in the church) Hussey was determined not to miss the chance of having a special piece of music written for the anniversary. He might have turned to an older composer like Herbert Howells, a specialist in English church music whose carol 'A Spotless Rose' the Northampton choir sang and liked. But he wanted to find a composer who had not yet formed a known style in church music: who had not written much of it, even, but was anxious to do so, and whose secular music had the kind of freshness of invention that might extend the boundaries of church art in the same way as would the work of Moore and Sutherland.

Walter Hussey now therefore sought another composer, and his choice fell on Britten. He had liked the *Sinfonia da Requiem*, heard in a broadcast performance. He had also been impressed by a 'personal choice' BBC programme in which Britten's chosen music had included the 'Agnus Dei' from Verdi's *Requiem* and Mozart's 'Ave verum corpus', of which Britten had said that he was only beginning to understand it and found it more and more marvellous as he got to know it better; it so happened that this Mozart piece was Walter Hussey's favourite anthem. He wrote to Britten about his proposed commission, care of the BBC, and was not deterred by a cool response from Boosey & Hawkes, to whom the letter had been forwarded and who had taken it upon themselves to open it and reply, to the effect that Mr Britten was away ill in the country and that it was doubtful whether he would accept a Northampton commission. 'I was entirely re-stored,' Hussey recalls today, 'because the next thing I got was a letter in his own handwriting from the Old Mill at Snape.' Hussey had in his letter apologised for having a 'bee in his bonnet' about a close connection between the Church and the arts. Now Britten replied; 'Dear Mr Hussey, ... As I also have a "bee" about closer connection between the arts & the Church, I am sure that I shall have an idea before next September for an anthem for your jubilee.' He went to Northampton soon after to hear the church choir, listening also to four solo singers for whom he thought he might write.

Britten found rather an exceptional text for the Northampton piece in 'Rejoice in the Lamb', a long poem by the eighteenth-century poet Christopher Smart, who declined into madness and ended his days in an asylum. The work itself is rambling and eccentric, yet visionary and moving: having discovered it in a limited edition, the composer decided he could use certain passages for the Northampton celebration. Perhaps he was touched too by a remark in the introduction to Smart's poem (by William Stead) which attributed to the poet 'a child-like innocence, a bright celestial vision, a heart that was always affectionate, and a faith which survived years of misery and humiliation'; for the themes of innocence and the persecuted outsider are recurrent in Britten's work. That he caught the tone of the poem seems to be borne out by a later comment by the critic Scott Goddard in *British Music of our Time* (1946):

> *Rejoice in the Lamb* has about it a freshness unlike anything in our music, new in Britten's. The delicate steel-like tension of Christopher Smart's lines is echoed in music that has a similar quality of ageless youth and instinctive unquestioning wisdom. The effect, once it has registered upon the listener, is of music reaching the understanding with a vague, hesitant, yet quite vital touch as from some unexplored region of the mind.

Imogen Holst calls it 'as unlike conventional church music as it could possibly be', but although a slow earnestness was characteristic of most Anglican music, her own father Gustav Holst had written quick 'dancing' music in his *Hymn of Jesus* which Britten may have half-remembered when writing similar sections in his work. Nevertheless, the *Hymn of Jesus* is a concert piece, and Britten had brought a youthful vitality into the church itself was with the *con brio* and *vivace* markings of his score. *Rejoice in the Lamb* is essentially a work expressing praise and an affirmation of faith. It ends with a gently canonic final chorus – 'Hallelujah from the heart of God,/and from the hand of the artist inimitable' – that with its *ritmico* dotted rhythms owes much to Purcell. Though new and challenging, it is neither *outré* nor too hard for an amateur choir; it quite fulfils Britten's promise to Walter Hussey that it 'would offend no one who did not think that church music came to an end with Parry and Stanford'. He himself conducted the first performance on 21 September 1943.

Walter Hussey was to remain a friend. Britten composed one more piece for St Matthew's Church, in 1946, as Hussey recalls: 'We used to greet the Bishop, when he arrived at the west door of the church for our annual festival service, with Victoria's *Ecce sacerdos*. But this was not long enough to allow the procession to get to the sanctuary, so Ben wrote us a piece for organ to fill the gap, the Prelude and Fugue on a Theme of Victoria, the only organ piece he wrote. I was told he composed it in bed one morning, then got up and wrote it down.'

There was one occasion when Peter Pears and he came to

Northampton to give a recital. Britten had been ill; nevertheless the two men drove all the way from Suffolk in the composer's car, which at this time was an open Bristol tourer. 'He arrived absolutely wrapped up in everything, looking like death, with flasks of coffee and whisky – came in and demanded that every window be shut and all the fires turned on. He was really dreadful up to the time of the concert: gloomy, untalkative and so on. And then he went and played magnificently, of course – and came back a totally different person. He was bright, and cheerful; and we had supper. After supper I said, if you'll forgive me, I must just go over and visit the Saturday night dance. This was the regular Saturday night old-time dancing; a lot of people used to go. And Ben said, "I'll come with you!" I remember Peter saying, "Oh, is that wise, Ben?" "Yes!", said Ben, "Yes!" And he jumped up, and Peter said, just like a nanny, "Well, put on your overcoat when you go." It was a night that he plainly ought to. He said, "No, no, I shan't put on my overcoat" – but I think he *did*, fortunately. Then he walked over to this "hop", with every conceivable age of person there – simple, humble people – and was marvellous. I left him! He walked round the room talking to all the people, they loving him and he loving it too – looking and seeming the picture of health.'

There were other musical occasions too. Britten said that if the St Matthew's choir would learn Verdi's *Stabat Mater* he would come and conduct it – and did; and he and Pears once visited the parish Junior School unexpectedly and informally and delighted the children there with some songs.

There was another vocal work that occupied Britten during that summer of 1943, especially after he had put the finishing touches to *Rejoice in the Lamb* in mid-July. This was the *Serenade* for tenor, horn and strings. It is undoubtedly one of the most significant among his compositions of the immediately post-American period, which were predominantly vocal pieces to English words that served, consciously or otherwise, as preparation for the projected opera *Peter Grimes*: we know that, since his schooldays, it had been characteristic for him to plan ahead methodically and also to stand back and view his art in the long term. There was another stimulus too, equally typical of him and complementary rather than contradictory – a request for a piece from a performer known to him. This was Dennis Brain: a horn player of exceptional ability and already widely recognised (at twenty-two) as a master of his instrument. What he asked Britten for was the obvious thing, a concerto. But as we have seen, this did not fit into the composer's scheme of things at the time. Instead Britten produced a vocal cycle with string orchestra, as *Les Illuminations* had been, but with the important extra element of an obbligato horn solo part that rises both technically and interpretatively to concerto dimensions; to take one example only, the fifth of the six song settings (Jonson's 'Hymn to Diana', the huntress goddess) is a scherzo for voice and horn alike. The horn also has the privilege of framing the whole work with an unaccompanied prologue and epilogue played on the 'natural' notes of the instrument.

The *Serenade* is a small anthology of poems on the subject of evening, finding its unity in this way rather than by the more usual use of a single author. Britten chose his texts with skill to provide a variety and sequence of moods, and thus his music may be fast or slow, calm or disturbed (even alarming, as in the anonymous fifteenth-century dirge, 'This Ae Nighte') without ever departing from the vespertine theme; this is evening in substance as well as picturesque surface. The author and critic Edward Sackville-West, to whom the work is dedicated, wrote of it perceptively:

> The subject is Night and its prestigia: the lengthening shadow, the distant bugle at sunset, the Baroque panoply of the starry sky, the heavy angels of sleep; but also the cloak of evil – the worm in the heart of the rose, the sense of sin in the heart of man.

Critical opinion has always been favourable to the *Serenade* following upon its Wigmore Hall première on 15 October 1943 with Peter Pears, Dennis Brain and a string orchestra conducted by Walter Goehr. (The recording made the following May has Britten himself conducting the Boyd Neel Orchestra with the same soloists.) A decade after its composition, the *Times* critic Frank Howes was still to refer to it as 'an epitome of Britten's art ... immediately captivating and permanently satisfying'. Ten years later still, in the *London Magazine* for October 1963,

Norman Del Mar called it 'the noble Serenade, still considered by many to be Britten's most inspired creation'. As usual, Britten himself tried to maintain a sense of proportion about his achievement and critical success, even when friends spoke excitedly about a 'rebirth' of English music. In a letter to Imogen Holst written a few days after the première of the *Serenade*, he wrote:

> It is encouraging that you too sense that 'something' in the air which heralds a renaissance. I feel terrifically conscious of it. Whether we are the voices crying in the wilderness or the thing itself it isn't for us to know, but anyhow it is so very exciting. It is of course in all the arts, but in music, particularly, it's this acceptance of 'freedom' without any arbitrary restrictions, this simplicity, this contact with audiences of our own time and of people like ourselves, this seriousness, and above all this professionalism.

One notices that Britten writes of 'we' and 'us'. He would not allow extravagant compliments to go to his head. Nor did he think of himself as the only important new voice in music. He was both a friend and collaborator of other composers. He played Lennox Berkeley's two-piano music, as well as his own, in concert with Clifford Curzon, at the Wigmore Hall in March 1944, and he also partnered Francis Poulenc in the French composer's Concerto for Two Pianos at the Royal Albert Hall in January 1945. Another composer friend was Michael Tippett, then teaching at Morley College. Tippett asked Peter Pears to sing at this London college for adult students and then wrote his cantata *Boyhood's End* for Pears and Britten, which they performed at Morley in June 1943. Two weeks later Tippett, who like Pears and Britten was a pacifist, was imprisoned for three months at Wormwood Scrubs for failing to comply with the conditions of his exemption from military or other service. It so happened that the two artists were booked to give a prison concert there, and Tippett recalls: 'I am ashamed to mention the untruthful wangling by which I convinced the authorities that the recital was impossible unless I turned the pages for the pianist. Up to the last moment it was touch and go. But finally I stepped out of the ranks and sat down unexpectedly at the piano beside him. A strange moment for us both.' After Tippett was released from the Scrubs, it was Britten who helped him mount a performance of his oratorio *A Child of Our Time*. Three of the four soloists came from Sadler's Wells, Pears, Joan Cross and Owen Brannigan – 'an imperfect première under execrable conditions', Tippett has written, 'but inescapably moving.'

Peter Pears had since 1943 been a member of the Sadler's Wells Company; and Britten too was at this time close to the artists for whom the opera *Peter Grimes* was to be written. He had finished 1943 with incidental music to *The Rescue*, a radio play by Edward Sackville-West based on part of the *Odyssey*, and a 'Ballad of Little Musgrave and Lady Barnard' for male voices with piano, written for friends in a German prisoner-of-war camp and sent to them there via the censor. Both these pieces, otherwise so different, were dramatic. The same vivid quality had already been apparent in the *Serenade*, of which the critic Percy Young wrote, 'This is dramatic music . . . A composer who can show such tension is half-way to becoming an opera composer.' And Britten's incidental music for film, theatre and radio, together with such 'dramatic' instrumental works as the *Sinfonia da Requiem*, had provided invaluable experience for a future composer of opera. So had the substantial list of vocal works written over a ten-year period, from *A Boy was Born* to *Rejoice in the Lamb*. He had even had the opportunity – and taken it in good measure – of trying his hand in his (at least relatively) prentice work for the opera house, *Paul Bunyan*, whose failure he could leave behind him on the other side of the Atlantic together with much of the Auden ethos and experience. The *Peter Grimes* text had been taking shape over the 1942–43 period. Now it was ready for his music. As we have seen in Chapter 1, all of 1944 was spent on the composition of *Grimes*, the composition sketch being finished in February 1945.

Though *Peter Grimes* has already been extensively discussed in Chapter 1, perhaps one additional comment may be made here. The musico-dramatic skill of the opera, which brought the work an instant success and established it (and its composer) in the international repertory, is the very opposite of surprising. A first full-scale opera it may be, but it must be admitted that Britten was exceptionally well prepared for its composition. Even before the première and the subsequent wave of triumph which was to carry him forward, he had written in the Sadler's Wells Opera Book No. 3 of the future of opera in Great Britain, describing it as 'the most exciting of musical forms'. Of *Grimes*, almost in passing he used the words 'Whatever its reception may be' – of course *Paul Bunyan* had failed – but now there was a quiet confidence: 'I wanted to write more works for the stage.' *Peter Grimes*, in June 1945, marked the real beginning of his operatic career. After that, the opera always drew him. Nevertheless, it is worth remembering that when Charles Osborne interviewed Britten in 1963 for the *London Magazine* and said, 'I think of you as primarily an operatic composer', Britten interrupted to remark, 'Well, I don't know that I do. Certainly I respond very deeply to words, but not necessarily only opera'; and he went on to mention his pleasure in a new and purely instrumental work, the Cello Symphony. We should not think of him as essentially an operatic, or even a vocal composer, but try to maintain a more balanced picture. Nevertheless the following chapters will show opera, in its wider sense of musical drama, as a recurrent and important theme in his subsequent creative life.

6

From Glyndebourne
to East Anglia (1946–48)

Allegro molto
MAYOR

The re-per-cussions of this Fes-ti-val   will travel far, wide, deep

____ and strong,

Albert Herring, Act II

As Peter Pears remembers, Britten was 'very excited and pleased, no question about that' with the success of *Peter Grimes*. And not only had the opera itself succeeded: more than this, its extraordinary impact seemed to mark a revitalisation of English music that was sorely needed. (The renaissance of music in these islands had begun late in the nineteenth century and included several major figures, but by 1945 it was clearly running out of steam: William Walton, in his early forties, had not sustained his brilliant youthful creativity, while Vaughan Williams, though still creatively active, was elderly.) Britten was thrilled to feel needed in England. With the ending of the war his pacifism was no longer a sore point and this was one tension removed; there were still mutterings about his private life and envious hints (never supported by evidence) that he owed his success merely to the backing of 'wealthy patrons', but these were now more muted than hitherto. By and large, the tide had turned, and Britten was established and accepted as a major figure. Though young, he had served a long apprenticeship. (In fact he was exactly the same age as Schubert when he died in 1828.) He was now far more confident and ready to face the future. As Edward Sackville-West wrote in 1945:

A good opera ... represents the composer at the height of his powers: it must always be a result, never a point of departure (except for future operas). It is a bourne from which the traveller may return, but with an outlook necessarily changed by the experience.

Perhaps always from this time onwards, Britten found himself to be consciously an Englishman, both musically and personally – if, as has already been suggested, the distinction is valid in his case. The Old Mill at Snape remained his home, from which the Welfords (his sister Beth's family) moved out after the war. He and Pears also kept a *pied-à-terre* in London, save for a short period around 1947, which was convenient for concerts and meeting and visits to the dentist; and though they changed addresses occasionally they found they needed something of the kind throughout their joint career. But as for composition, his rule, at least for many years, was that 'I only write while I am at home' – and that meant Suffolk, at first in Snape and then later in Aldeburgh. The Englishness of his environment was reflected in a series of works, for example the settings of folk song melodies that he made for Peter Pears and himself to perform in recitals.

Pears has written illuminatingly on these 'folk' pieces, which occupied Britten at intervals throughout his life.

Benjamin Britten first started arranging folk songs for the concerts which he and I gave together in America during the War and, when we returned to England, for CEMA and Friends War Relief. They made a very good end to a programme which started with Purcell, went on with Schubert and included one of Britten's Cycles. He made something like forty arrangements for voice with either piano, guitar or harp. The folk-song revival, which started around the turn of the century, was already more or less a thing of the past when Britten was composing in the early thirties, and it had very little effect on his music. He himself found the manifestations of the Movement rather tiresome and certainly could not see himself using folk song as part of the structure of his music. His teacher, Frank Bridge, was not sympathetic to the ideals of the composers taking part and Britten was not encouraged in that direction. It was not therefore to the volumes of the English Folk Song Society that Britten went for his tunes and texts in the first years. He found a little, old, charmingly-printed book of National Melodies collected by the Victorian composer and teacher, John Hullah. In this book there were some so-called folk songs which Cecil Sharp would have thrown out. But Britten took up many of them and 'The Ash Grove' comes from this, so does 'There's none to soothe' and several others.

His way with a folk-song is very different from that of Cecil Sharp who arranged so many for schools in the first part of the century: one of Sharp's cherished ideas was to bring back to English children those tunes that had been sung to and by their ancestors and he used to arrange these songs for voice and piano with very simple and regularly barred accompaniment. This would not do for Britten. He wanted to recreate these melodies with their texts for concert performances, to make them art-songs, in the tradition of Schubert and even Brahms. He therefore takes the tune as if he had written it himself and thinks himself back as to how he would turn it into a song. The result is sometimes artfully simple and almost folk-song-like ('Salley Gardens', 'Waly, Waly', 'The Foggy Dew'), sometimes more elaborate and sophisticated ('The Ash Grove', 'Early one morning') and still others have an accompaniment of a strong pattern which could reasonably be called Schubertian (many of the French and Irish songs).

This lengthy quotation from Peter Pears makes it clear that Britten was not of the generation of the nationalists, represented above all by Vaughan Williams; even before him, composers such as Arthur Bliss and William Walton (Frank Bridge too) had moved away from nationalism towards a more consciously cosmopolitan outlook. But he did not need to repudiate folk song as Bliss and Walton had done. Rather, he came to it with imagination and affection, as a creative artist rather than a merely respectful scholar. Frank Howes' view of these folk song settings, in the 1954 Fifth Edition of *Grove's Dictionary*, is fairly typical of critical comment upon them in the forties and fifties:

that there are 'some strained examples, but others show once again ... (his) extraordinary mixture of sophisticated ingenuity with simplicity of effect'.

If there was something ambivalent about Britten's attitude to the folk song tradition – or at any rate the folk song 'movement' – there was none as regards Purcell and the tradition of English vocal music, both secular and sacred, that stemmed from him. He had been attracted to Purcell while at the Royal College, and though he knew only a few Purcell songs in the 1930s, that knowledge came in full measure through performances of them with Peter Pears. In the late 1940s he made several Purcell realisations, which were arrangements with the keyboard part filled out from the original figured bass and designed for a modern piano rather than the harpsichord (twenty years later they would certainly have been composed for the older instrument): not so very different, really, from the technique of the folk song arrangements where he was also proceeding afresh from a given melody. In the early sixties Britten was to say to Murray Schafer: 'Purcell is a great master at handling the English language in song, and I learned much from him. I recall a critic once asking me from whom I had learned to set English poetry to music. I told him Purcell; he was amazed. I suppose he expected me to say folk music and Vaughan Williams ... (my) First Canticle was ... certainly modelled on the Purcell *Divine Hymns*; but few people knew their Purcell well enough to realise that.' He went on to mention his excursions into texts in languages other than English and to relate these also to the practice of his great predecessor: 'I am sure Purcell felt the same way in his own day about this, for surely he was influenced by French and Italian music too.' (So, we may note in passing, was J. S. Bach.) In 1952 Donald Mitchell was to cite – though only in order to refute it – the view of Britten that 'lying outside nationalist musical considerations he fails to secure a place for himself in our affections'. Britten, as his whole work demonstrates, was 'national' without being 'nationalist' in the folk-orientated way of Vaughan Williams in England, Falla in Spain or even Gershwin in America. His music is English in the same way as that of Bach and Beethoven are German.

For all its musical eclecticism, *Peter Grimes* was essentially

English in this way, true to the harsher as well as the softer elements of Crabbe's poem, to the East Anglian land- and sea-scape and its coastal weather, to the popular institutions of pub or church. A setting of mattins, off-stage, accompanies the crucial scene of Act II between Ellen, the young apprentice and later Peter Grimes. And the composition of *Grimes* was followed in 1945 by a short Anglican liturgical work, a *Festival Te Deum* written for the centenary of St Mark's Church, Swindon. The religious theme, and the 'English' one, were to be continued in a new vocal cycle written for Peter Pears and himself to perform, *The Holy Sonnets of John Donne*. The cycle was performed for the first time by Pears and Britten on the composer's birthday, 22 November 1945, at the Wigmore Hall in London, while on the preceding day, there had been the première of an instrumental work of an equally strong Englishness, the Second String Quartet written to commemorate the 250th anniversary of the death of Purcell and whose finale bears the Purcellian title (and form) of chacony.

The account of the conception and composition of the *Donne Sonnets*, which was given on different occasions by both Britten and Pears, is in several respects significant. It reminds us first of the composer's responsiveness to his environment, and second of his proneness to illness and uncanny ability to turn even ill-health to creative advantage. The theme of these poems provides a counterpart to the *Michelangelo Sonnets*, which had discussed love; here the subject-matter is death, sin and redemption. This was also, effectively, to be the theme of Britten's next opera, *The Rape of Lucretia*. The idea for the *Donne Sonnets* was already germinating in the composer's mind when, in the summer of 1945, he asked the violinist Yehudi Menuhin if he could go with him on a recital tour of German concentration camps. The two musicians played to liberated prisoners, men and women in an appalling state of privation, who were awaiting the authorities' aid to return to their homes after medical care restored them sufficiently to travel. 'We gave two or three short recitals a day – they couldn't take more,' Britten recalled. On his return from Germany he suffered a delayed reaction from an inoculation administered before his departure. The nine *Sonnets*, as he tells us, were written 'in a week while in bed with a high fever'. On

10 August, a day or so before starting work on them, he had written to his friend Jean Maud:

> I'm in bed, & *ever* so sorry for myself (infantile things like vaccinations can be horrible when you're a hoary old man). . . . Germany was a terrific & horrific experience; eminently worth while. I'm trying to get similar parties to repeat the dose, because it *is* necessary. I'm getting Unrra [the United Nations Relief and Rehabilitation Administration], Brit. Council etc. on to it. Too much to write about in my present feeble state (anyhow this letter must be hell to read) – but I'll tell all about when we meet . . . Yehudi was nice, & what's more a sport, which was the quality most needed on the trip.

The letter is both personal and practical, keeping the experience in proportion; he was amused, for example, by an official misdescription of himself as 'Mr Button, Mr Menuhin's secretary'. But his musical imagination worked at a different level, and though the *Sonnets* were planned before his departure, it is hard to believe, as Pears has written, 'that the horrors of Belsen did not have some direct impact on the creative unconscious'. The composer himself said later: 'I think the connection between personal experience and my feelings about the poetry was a strong one. It certainly characterised the music.' The last *Donne Sonnet*, called 'Death, be not proud', is a Purcellian passacaglia in a strong B major tonality. To quote Pears again, 'Death has been conquered, not by an old man who waits for it resigned and patient, but on the contrary by a still young one who defies the nightmare horror with a strong love, the instinctive answer to Buchenwald from East Anglia.'

Britten's success with *Peter Grimes* had naturally aroused curiosity as to what sort of opera he would write next. As Edward Sackville-West recognised, *Grimes* might serve as a 'point of departure' for new operas. In fact Britten was to compose three more operas within the four-year period following the *Grimes* première: *The Rape of Lucretia*, *Albert Herring* and *The Little Sweep*. However, none of these was in any sense 'grand' opera, with large orchestra and chorus, as *Grimes* had been; and the reason for this, at least initially, had nothing to do with art. 'Whether we would have moved away from big-scale opera had Joan

[Cross] stayed at Sadler's Wells is a question possibly worth debating,' Peter Pears remembers. 'I mean, certainly we left, partly for personal reasons, partly because the atmosphere had got not very friendly, and also because it was the end of the war and I suppose it was time for changes anyway. Joan had done her stint and the governors (Edward Dent was one of them) called Clive Carey in to take control; I suppose they thought generally that the company wasn't in a very good state. Joan was, in fact, really asked to go. Maybe it was time that she did, in the sense that she didn't want to stay. But it then meant that our loyalties to her really made us forsake Sadler's Wells.' What happened was that a number of the Sadler's Wells singers banded together to demand artistic control in place of Tyrone Guthrie and Joan Cross, refusing to sign new contracts unless they got their way, and the governors accepted their ultimatum. Clearly there was no future at the Wells for Joan Cross, who left the company in 1945, not long after the *Peter Grimes* première. Peter Pears followed her; and so did two others associated with *Grimes*, Eric Crozier and Reginald Goodall.

Despite this setback, Eric Crozier tells us that Britten was 'immensely eager' to write more operas. But where were they to be produced? The Covent Garden Opera had not yet reopened, though it was to do so in 1946 and then to mount Tyrone Guthrie's production of *Peter Grimes* in its 1947–48 season. Fortunately the private opera house of John and Audrey Christie (the soprano Audrey Mildmay) at Glyndebourne in Sussex came to the rescue. The Glyndebourne theatre was small but well-equipped, seating a mere six hundred persons, who paid accordingly high prices for their seats but knew that the theatre's policy was to provide unsparingly high quality. Like Sadler's Wells and Covent Garden, Glyndebourne had been closed during the war, but it was to reopen in 1946. Their general manager Rudolf Bing supported the idea of mounting a new Britten opera, and the Christies agreed to set up a new opera company, the Glyndebourne English Opera Company. Britten's new opera, *The Rape of Lucretia*, was to be presented there in the summer of 1946. It was to be a chamber opera, using eight singers and an orchestra (or ensemble) of twelve instrumentalists.

Eric Crozier had lent Britten his copy of André Obey's play

Le viol de Lucrèce. He in turn passed it on to the poet Ronald Duncan, a friend of Britten's who had written the text of his *Pacifist March* in 1937 and for whose verse play *This Way to the Tomb* Britten had provided incidental music. It was agreed that Duncan should write the libretto, which was also to draw upon Shakespeare's treatment of the same subject; John Piper was to design and Crozier was to produce. Piper was Britten's choice; though they had not worked together before, they had known each other from pre-war days and shared the view that an opera composer, librettist and designer should, in Britten's words, 'be working in the closest contact, from the most preliminary stages right up to the first night'. Two casts, and two conductors were chosen for the production, since fourteen performances had to be given within two weeks. The two Lucretias were Kathleen Ferrier and Nancy Evans, while Peter Pears and Joan Cross (doubling with Aksel Schiøtz and Flora Nielsen) were to sing the Male and Female Chorus who act from stage left and right as Christian commentators upon the pre-Christian quasi-historical story. Britten and Duncan had at first wondered who might be available to play the contralto title role, but the composer had liked Kathleen Ferrier's voice when he had heard it some months before and, as Duncan has written, they auditioned her:

> She was so terrified she could only whisper. We wondered how she could possibly sing ... He cut the talk to a minimum and handed her the score. She read it through once, then went to the piano and sang part of the Spinning Aria. We were both so moved by the quality of the voice that neither of us spoke. I had been impressed, too, by the genuine feeling of purity which came over. This was a very necessary quality for the part ... We had been extremely lucky. She was not only vocally perfect but it could not have been better casting from my point of view.

According to Duncan, the final preparations for *Lucretia* were tense:

> Everybody became very nervous as we approached the first night of the opera at Glyndebourne; so much depended on it. It was the first new opera to be presented there. Kathleen

Ferrier had some reason to be nervous: it was her first appearance on a stage. A feud had arisen between the producer, Eric Crozier, and Rudolf Bing, the Glyndebourne manager. Ben himself was making Christie a target for all his nervous tension. The peace was only kept by the extraordinary tact of two people, Audrey Christie and Ernest Ansermet. The night before the first performance I dreamed that Christie had told us all to leave Glyndebourne.

Musically, at least, matters were in good hands. The performances were directed by Reginald Goodall and the distinguished Swiss conductor Ernest Ansermet, who amused some of the cast by addressing the youthful composer respectfully (and in his view correctly) as '*maître*'.

The Rape of Lucretia disappointed some critics. Clearly it was not a powerful *verismo* opera with mass effects as *Grimes* had been – though this could hardly have been expected at Glyndebourne with its small stage and auditorium. The *Times* special correspondent was by no means alone in finding that the 'Christian moral tacked on' to the story struck a false note and indeed constituted a 'grave dramatic error'. It was mainly the libretto rather than the music that disturbed, and even the sympathetic Edward Sackville-West wrote of 'inappropriate jokes, absurd anachronisms.' Perhaps people were unaware that the framing anachronistic commentary had its respected precedent in Stravinsky's *Oedipus Rex* – a work which Britten had called 'one of the peaks of Stravinsky's output ... satisfying every aesthetic demand'. But at any rate, the music of *Lucretia* was admired, the *Times* critic finding 'a very sure touch ... the age-old balance of music and drama is struck anew' and describing the lullaby for the sleeping Lucretia as 'extremely beautiful'. By October 1947 the opera had received a hundred performances and had also been recorded in an abridged version incorporating revisions mainly to do with the libretto. Performances had taken place not only at Glyndebourne but also in London and five provincial cities, and (at the invitation of the Dutch Wagner Society) in Holland. The English provincial tour played to poor houses, though, and cost John Christie about £14,000; Britten later remembered tensions and the gentle-natured Kathleen

Ferrier smoothing things over by telling him to 'be *nice*!'. As for the general reception of the opera, the composer wrote to an understanding friend, Imogen Holst:

> ... the manner in which you approach the Christian idea delighted me. I used to think that the day when one could shock people was over – but now, I've discovered that being simple and considering things spiritual of importance produces violent reactions!

Immediately after the Glyndebourne production of *Lucretia*, Britten made a brief visit to America to attend the United States première of *Peter Grimes*. Performances of the opera were given on 6–8 August 1946 at the Berkshire Music Centre presided over by Serge Koussevitzky at Tanglewood, Massachusetts. Koussevitzky, as we have seen, had commissioned the opera four years previously, though he had then generously waived his rights to the world première; he was present at the American first performance but did not himself conduct the work, leaving this to his former assistant at Tanglewood, the twenty-seven-year-old Leonard Bernstein. It may have been pleasant for Britten to revisit the United States as a fêted figure. Wystan Auden made a point of getting to Tanglewood to see *Grimes*: there is a photograph of him and Britten amiably chatting. Perhaps they had time to catch up on gossip about mutual friends, not the least interesting item of which must have been that Auden was enjoying a heterosexual affair with an attractive divorcee, Rhoda Jaffe, concurrently with his flexible though lasting relationship with Chester Kallman! Auden wrote to Rhoda: 'it was fine to see Benjy Britten again. The performance was terrible but the work made an impression just the same.' Britten's own comments are not recorded; Pears does not remember him thinking the performance a bad one, and he looks happy enough standing with Eric Crozier (who produced) on stage at the curtain call. *Peter Grimes* was to reach the prestigious Metropolitan Opera House in New York eighteen months later, on 12 February 1948. Four days later *Time* splashed a picture of 'Britain's Britten' on its cover and printed a substantial article on him under the title 'Opera's New Face'. The composer was referred to throughout as 'Benjy', a diminutive Auden used;

however, when I asked him not very long afterwards if it was
generally employed he said that it was not, save perhaps by his
family and a few early friends. (I had been introduced to Britten
by Lennox Berkeley, at this time my composition professor at
the Royal Academy of Music.)

On returning from America, Britten composed an Occasional
Overture in C major for the BBC to mark the opening of the
BBC Third Programme on 29 September 1946. The new Third
Programme was, in the music administrator Julian Herbage's
proud words, 'entirely devoted to broadcasts of a cultural
nature'; it survives today as the largely music-carrying Radio 3.
Britten finished his Overture a fortnight before the broadcast
opening concert; but he was dissatisfied with the piece and
withdrew it after this performance. The present writer recalls it
as lively and athletic; the score still exists and doubtless it will
eventually be heard again. Another commissioned work proved
to be a great deal more durable. This was the music he composed
in the early autumn of 1946 for the Crown Film Unit's documentary and educational film, *The Instruments of the Orchestra*.
For this film he wrote a lively set of *Variations and figure on a
theme of Purcell* that featured the orchestral instruments singly
and in groups; in the final fugue they all entered in turn. Eric
Crozier provided an explanatory spoken commentary, but this
is nearly always omitted today in concert performances, where
the piece is more properly called *The Young Person's Guide to
the Orchestra*. It was heard in concert, in fact, even before the
film was shown in November 1946: the first performance took
place on 15 October under Malcolm Sargent in Liverpool with
the Liverpool Philharmonic Orchestra. Since that time it has
probably been the composer's most popular single work. This is
not surprising, for it is exuberant and uncomplicated music,
scored with clarity and vigour.

The extroverted qualities of *The Young Person's Guide to the
Orchestra* can, however, make us overlook the fact that it fits
well into Britten's *oeuvre*. For one thing, the use of a Purcell
theme is characteristic. So is the dedication to four children, the
children of his friends John and Jean Maud. On 8 January 1947
he wrote to Jean Maud from a skiing holiday among 'the snows
of Zermatt' suggesting the wording of the dedication to Hum-

phrey, Pamela, Caroline and Virginia Maud 'for their edification & entertainment'. A less-known fact is that the ebullient *Young Person's Guide* is also, at least in part, one of his several *in memoriam* pieces; for Pamela Maud had died five years previously. This collaboration with Eric Crozier (as a writer, not a producer) was to lead to other 'young persons'' pieces. His next opera, *Albert Herring*, the cantata *Saint Nicolas* and *The Little Sweep* all have children's roles and Crozier texts.

Britten was now in his early thirties, and exceptionally busy, with the problems of a busy man who must decide on priorities. He had his concert work with Peter Pears, artistically fruitful but time-consuming especially when they travelled abroad, as they did in Europe in the seasons of 1945–6 and 1946–7 (when they gave recitals in Holland, Belgium, Scandinavia and Switzerland). He was now also a conductor, directing performances of his *Young Person's Guide* and *Serenade*. Besides these things, he was, together with John Piper and Eric Crozier, to become an artistic director of a new company, the English Opera Group. In the meantime John Christie asked Ronald Duncan and Britten to write another chamber opera for Glyndebourne. Something lighter than *Lucretia* was wanted, so an Abélard and Héloïse theme was rejected – Britten had already seen the difficulty of the hero's castration and asked if a baritone could possibly sing countertenor in Act II! – and another proposed Duncan libretto for Jane Austen's *Mansfield Park* with roles for Ferrier and Pears had not worked out satisfactorily. Indeed Duncan's star seems to have been in decline during this period. By contrast, his other collaborator Eric Crozier was proving gifted and congenial. It was he who had originally suggested the *Lucretia* story, as we have seen. Now, when he put forward the idea of making a Guy de Maupassant short story into a comic opera, Britten asked him to write the libretto himself. The result was *Albert Herring*, first performed in June 1947 by the English Opera Group at Glyndebourne.

A 'companion and contrast to *The Rape of Lucretia*', as Crozier calls it, *Albert Herring* used a similar twelve-piece orchestra and small company of singers and could also be toured not too expensively. The announcement of the new opera formed part of an English Opera Group manifesto dating from early in

1947, headed by several distinguished names besides those of Britten, Crozier and Piper, the founders; among these were Oliver Lyttleton, Kenneth Clark, Tyrone Guthrie and Ralph Hawkes. The new company's aims were stated as follows:

> We believe the time has come when England, which has never had a tradition of native opera, but has always depended upon a repertory of foreign works, can create its own operas. Opera is as much a vital means of artistic expression as orchestral music, drama and painting. The lack of it has meant a certain impoverishment of English artistic life. We believe the best way to achieve the beginnings of a repertory of English operas is through the creation of a form of opera requiring small resources of singers and players, but suitable for performance in large or small opera houses or theatres. A first essay in this direction was the writing and staging of Britten's *The Rape of Lucretia* in 1946. *Lucretia* was an experiment towards finding a flexible and sensitive operatic form built on the collaboration of small numbers of singers, musicians and other artists. *Lucretia* was given 80 performances in 1946 – more performances than any other British opera has had in its first season, with two exceptions, since the beginning of the century. The success of this experiment has encouraged the three persons chiefly involved – Benjamin Britten, the composer; Eric Crozier, the producer; and John Piper, the designer – to continue their work as a group by establishing, under their artistic direction, a new opera company to be known as THE ENGLISH OPERA GROUP, incorporated on a non-profit-making basis. This Group will give annual seasons of contemporary opera in English and suitable classical works including those of Purcell. It is part of the Group's purpose to encourage young composers to write for the operatic stage, also to encourage poets and playwrights to tackle the problem of writing libretti in collaboration with composers.

The support of leading singers and players, the manifesto went on, was assured, and the conductors would be Britten and Reginald Goodall. An appeal for funds was made to supplement promised Arts Council money: £10,000 was needed. As for present plans, 'Benjamin Britten is now writing his third opera

– *Albert Herring*, a comedy about life in a Suffolk village. It is scored for 12 singers and 12 players ... (and) will open at Glyndebourne on June 20th.'

Albert Herring was first thought of in October 1946, with eight months to go before the curtain rose on its première; during this period Britten, Crozier and Piper had to write and design the work, raise money for the production and its following tour, engage singers, orchestra and technicians, book theatres and publicise their plans. Fortunately they acted swiftly and surely in all these spheres. The story was Maupassant's *Le Rosier de Madame Husson* ('Madame Husson's Rose-bush'), written in 1888 and set in the Normandy town of Gisors; it had already been made into a film with Fernandel as the greengrocer's boy. The decision to transport the action from Normandy to Suffolk was quickly made. Crozier's grandfather had kept a shop there, and the East Anglian background was also Britten's own. The 'small market-town' of Loxford was imaginary, (but there is a real Yoxford); however, with its Jubilee Hall and real outlying villages (Ufford, Orford, Iken, Snape and Campsey Ash) it might well be a smaller version of Aldeburgh – in fact Crozier calls it a town 'familiar to us both'. The story is of Albert Herring, the greengrocer's boy tied to his mother's apron-strings (she owns the shop) whose virtuous life causes him to be elected May King in default of suitably chaste girls who might have been chosen as Queen; he then kicks over the traces and goes off on a pub-crawling spree, so winning his independence to the delight of his contemporaries and the discomfiture of the pompous if well-meaning local worthies.

The first night of *Albert Herring*, on 20 June 1947 at Glyndebourne, went well enough, and launched the opera for a further forty or so performances during the rest of the year. There were dissenting critical voices, though, even if fewer than there had been with *Lucretia*, including some oddly snobbish reaction, it seems, to the idea of an opera about 'ordinary' people and set in a shop. (Even Figaro is of the servant class!) On the first night, John Christie met his Glyndebourne audience, according to Crozier, 'with an unhappy expression, saying "This isn't *our* kind of thing, you know" ... because it was in English he found it common.' And the *Times* critic must have forgotten who the librettist was when he told Crozier that he thought it 'a ghastly little work'. In print he was less rude, praising Frederick Ashton's production and the 'immense gusto' of the performance, in which Peter Pears played Albert and Joan Cross Lady Billows, but he expressed reservations – 'the animation of the comedy does not communicate itself to the listener because the music does not engage his heart. Mr Britten is still pursuing his old problem of seeing how much indigestible material he can dissolve in music ... the result is a charade.' The fundamental concept of chamber opera was also criticised as an unsatisfactory medium: 'Without the soft texture of a string foundation the rough edges of wind and percussion instruments impinge on the singers' vocal lines with harm to the delivery of the words. That the method itself and his brilliant use of it are original is beyond question, but it seems to be leading him up a blind alley.'

A warmer reaction to *Albert Herring* came from the critic Stephen Williams. His comments on the première of *Peter Grimes* have already been quoted; two years later, writing for the *Penguin Music Magazine*, he was still grudging in his praise, calling Britten 'a cult ... immensely successful and immensely fashionable ... I refuse to join in the almost hysterical adulation', though he had gone on to note the 'brilliant musicianship' and 'moving appeal' of *The Rape of Lucretia*. Now, after *Albert Herring*, he wrote of 'sparkling and ingenious music that is sometimes witty, sometimes idyllic ... we all enjoyed ourselves immensely, and agreed that if it was not great opera, it was at least good fun.' There was the usual sting in the tail, though: 'Now that Britten has got this out of his system, we wait for something worthier of his exceptional powers.' It was the same old story – no one denied the composer's skill, but the use to which it was put displeased some critics. Neville Cardus, in the *Manchester Guardian*, was rare in his unstinted praise for the opera's 'concentrated genius'.

After Glyndebourne, the English Opera Group toured the two chamber operas to Holland ('*Albert* was much to their taste,' Britten wrote) and Switzerland; they also performed Lennox Berkeley's *Stabat Mater*, written for the group and dedicated to Britten. It was then, while driving back by car across Europe, from the Lucerne Festival, that Peter Pears had what was to prove a historic idea. He suggested to Britten and Eric

Working on Peter Grimes*: Britten is at the piano, watched by Kenneth Green, the designer, Eric Crozier, the producer, and Reginald Goodall, the conductor of the first performance*

Peter Pears as Peter Grimes in the original production of the opera

Borough High Street, one of Kenneth Green's set designs for Peter Grimes

The Britten family. Benjamin, aged about 14, is on the right

Benjamin with Mr and Mrs Frank Bridge

Britten with W. H. Auden, photographed during work on Paul Bunyan *in New York*

Peter Pears and Benjamin Britten painted by Kenneth Green in 1943

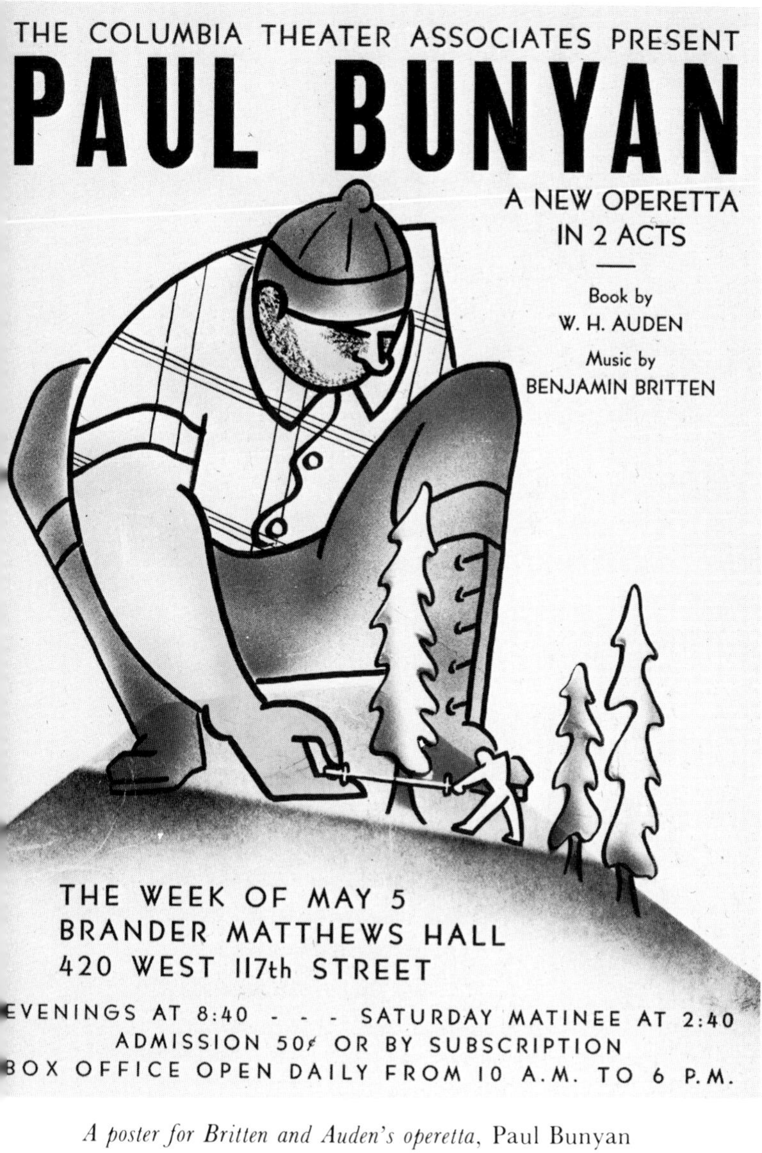

A poster for Britten and Auden's operetta, Paul Bunyan

Britten and Pears shopping in Aldeburgh High Street

The Maltings at Snape

Britten talking to Mr Squirrel, one of the cast, during rehearsals of Noye's Fludde *in 1958*

Our Hunting Fathers *in rehearsal at The Maltings in June 1976. With Britten are Peter Pears, André Previn and Elisabeth Söderström*

Britten in The Maltings foyer watching the filming of Owen Wingrave *for television*

Britten in Venice in 1975, with his nurse Rita Thompson (behind him, obscured)

Crozier: 'Why not make our own festival? A modest festival with a few concerts given by friends?' He and Britten had just moved into a house at Aldeburgh, Crag House on the sea front; so 'why not have an Aldeburgh Festival?' Pears asked. The idea was thoroughly discussed. After all, the cost of transporting opera (even chamber opera) from one city to another was very high; and despite good houses and British Council support this European tour would lose money and probably could not be repeated. Could the group instead persuade people to come to an English festival, in an East Anglian town, that was rather out of the way and with no special accommodation for music, just its church and the Jubilee Hall – a town where, at least in Crabbe's time, the locals were apt to 'scowl at strangers with suspicious eye'? All the pros and cons were gone over. Finally, Britten, Pears and Crozier agreed that if the Jubilee Hall at Aldeburgh proved big enough to accommodate some kind of simple operatic performances they would try to mount a festival there in 1948.

Back in England, these three planners hurried to Suffolk, talked to Aldeburgh's mayor and vicar who gave their preliminary approval to the festival scheme, and established a committee under the chairmanship of the Countess of Cranbrook. By January 1948 a public meeting had been held, and not long after this it was clear that some £2000 was already guaranteed (including £500 from the Arts Council) against the estimated festival expenses of £2500. The financial burden of providing the orchestra for three performances of *Albert Herring* was eased by Britten and Pears agreeing to give a recital in the Parish Church without taking a fee.

Preparations for the first Aldeburgh Festival of Music and the Arts went along briskly and optimistically, not only at the sophisticated artistic level but also in ways quite reminiscent of the First of May plans in *Albert Herring*'s Loxford, as Imogen Holst has described.

> Members of the local amateur dramatic society and the Women's Institute spent day after day addressing envelopes for the advance publicity; in the late spring fresh coats of paint appeared on many of the houses, and by the time it was June and the audiences began to arrive, the houses and shops

in the High Street had their window-ledges and balconies decorated with armfuls of flowers, including the beautiful yellow tree-lupins that still grow in profusion at the edge of the marshes.

Forster's 'bleak little place' really was setting itself out to welcome strangers. Forster himself was invited to give a festival lecture on Crabbe and *Peter Grimes* and found the Baptist Chapel 'painted up in cream and chocolate', and his friend William Plomer, the future librettist of *Gloriana* and the church parables, also came and lectured on Edward FitzGerald, like Crabbe a Suffolk literary figure.

The festival lasted a week and opened with a concert in the Parish Church whose chief item was Britten's cantata, *Saint Nicolas*, to a text by Eric Crozier. St Nicolas was one of the two patron saints of Lancing College in Sussex, Peter Pears's old school. Lancing was to celebrate its centenary in July 1948 and at the suggestion of Mrs Esther Neville-Smith, the widow of a college master and an old friend from Pears's schooldays, Britten had agreed (for a £100 commissioning fee) to compose a work for the occasion. The Lancing performance, conducted by the composer, was to take place on 24 July; Britten came in his open Rolls Royce tourer and soon made friends among the boys. (My vocal score of the work bears the inscription in Britten's writing: 'For Esther but for whom it would never have happened! – with our love' and is signed by 'Ben', 'Peter' and 'Eric'.) But in the meantime, by courtesy of Lancing College, the work had auspiciously opened the Aldeburgh Festival on 5 June, where for Forster 'the sudden contrast between elaborate singing and the rough breathy voices of three kids from a local "Co-op" made one swallow in the throat and water in the eyes. It was one of those triumphs outside the rules of art which only the great artist can achieve.' The critic Donald Mitchell, later Britten's publisher and friend, wrote: 'I was so confused by its progressively overwhelming impact that all I could find to say was: "This is too beautiful".'

Saint Nicolas falls into nine sections and tells the story of the fourth-century saint in dramatic, indeed almost operatic music; there is a charming and innocent waltz depicting his birth and childhood and a thrilling choral storm at sea, together with two English hymns (in which the audience, or congregation, joins) and a plainchant Nunc Dimittis as he dies. The saint's death, incidentally, is presented in a positive Christian way as the tenor soloist sings the words 'Lord, I come to life, to final birth'. And the hymn that follows, in which all join, 'God moves in a mysterious way' (the tune is 'London New' to Cowper's text), is wholly affirmative. Britten's harmonisation of the familiar melody, both here and in the other hymn, 'All people that on earth do dwell', is unorthodox but convincing, like that of his folk song arrangements. (At least to most people, though a respected academic composer complained about 'too many six-fours', i.e. second inversions of triads, chords treated in textbooks with kid gloves and by Britten with a master's sovereign freedom.)

The first Aldeburgh Festival was enough of a success for it to be clear by the end that it could be an annual event. E. M. Forster had attended the first of the three performances of *Albert Herring* in the Jubilee Hall; it seated under three hundred people, while on the little stage the children's ball game had to be played rather carefully. It was also 'excessively hot', Forster remembered. Yet somehow this was all part of the fun: 'It was delightful to burst out in the intervals on to the beach, or to watch the crowd who were partly in evening dress and partly dressed anyhow, and exempt from the drilled smartness of Glyndebourne. During the first interval a man in a pub said: "I took a ticket for this show because it is local and I felt I had to ... I wouldn't part with it now for ten pounds".'

In that summer of 1948, Britten was approaching his thirty-fifth birthday. Obviously he was still young; but it was a full fifteen years since he had left the Royal College of Music and begun. his career as a professional composer. He had, even though only partially, uprooted himself from his Suffolk background during those years, both physically and musically; but now he was again settled in Suffolk, living and working in the town of Aldeburgh which was henceforth to be his permanent home. His friendship and artistic collaboration with Peter Pears promised an equal permanence. He was an artistic director of the English Opera Group and a founder (with Pears and Crozier) of the Aldeburgh Festival. In other words his life was taking on its future pattern: that of a working composer (and performer) remaining in touch with a local community as well as the wider musical world. He was to say, 'I want to serve the community': and thus, although the tenor solo in *Saint Nicolas* is, in his own words, 'no amateur matter', most of the other performers are intended to be amateurs.

Saint Nicolas is a work that belongs in the tradition of the Anglican Church. This was not new in Britten – one remembers *A Boy was Born*, *A Ceremony of Carols* and *Rejoice in the Lamb* among other pieces – but its very nature makes it seem something like an affirmation of faith. Britten had gone as a boy with his parents to St John's Church at Lowestoft on Sundays. Can one say of him, as Charles Osborne has written of Wystan Auden, that 'it is hardly surprising that when, in his early thirties, he came to examine himself and his beliefs, he should discover that the faith drilled into him as a child had by no means died'? It would seem so, for his biographer Eric Walter White asserts, in a book whose text was authorised by the composer: 'His religious beliefs are central to his life and his work. As a devout and practising Christian, he has been keen, wherever possible, to work within the framework of the Church of England, and many of his compositions have been planned accordingly.' However, the facts now seem to be less simple. Britten was not a regular communicant or churchgoer. As Walter Hussey, by then the Dean of Chichester, said in the memorial address given in Westminster Abbey on 10 March 1977: 'Ben did not feel able to describe himself as an orthodox churchman.' Nevertheless he 'believed wholeheartedly in a power greater than the universe' and considered worship to be 'the ultimate purpose of all his art ... (he once said) "I am coming to feel more and more that *all* my music must be written to the glory of God".' Among later works, *Noye's Fludde*, the *War Requiem* and the three church parables are immediately obvious examples of music in which the composer seems to present a religious and moral statement. As he himself said of the *War Requiem*, 'the message is what counts'.

7

Aldeburgh and London (1949–53)

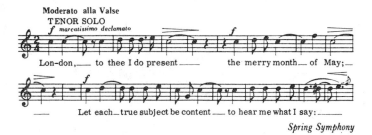

Moderato alla Valse
TENOR SOLO
f marcatissimo declamato

Lon-don,___ to thee I do present ___ the merry month___ of May;___

Let each___true subject be content ___ to hear me what I say:___

Spring Symphony

Eric Walter White, Britten's first biographer, considered that he reached complete musical maturity in his early thirties and that by 1948 'the full extent of his remarkable gifts had been revealed – the fluency, the protean variety, the feeling for effect, the love of setting words to music, and the deceptive simplicity of the melodic and harmonic means employed.' While agreeing with this, one should perhaps emphasise what is partly implied by White's mention of 'fluency', namely Britten's very workmanlike attitude to composing, writing to order and keeping to a tight time-schedule. 'I believe strongly in a routine,' the composer was to say in 1961. Much planning went on in his head, most often during regular afternoon walks with his dog, and then, if things went well, he could write quickly when he sat at his desk throughout the morning and again in the late afternoon. Imogen Holst has written of his orchestration in 1953 of the opera *Gloriana*, for which she prepared the pages for him as they sat side by side at separate tables: 'I was dismayed to see how quickly he wrote – he could get through twenty-eight pages in a day. I thought I should never catch up with him ... He seldom had to stop and think.'

If Britten's energy was formidable, so was his single-mindedness, as Imogen Holst recalls. There was 'one pouring wet day when he got soaked through while sitting indoors at his desk because he hadn't noticed that the rain was coming in on him'. But after his intense mental activity, he could be sad and tired. Once he asked Imogen Holst, 'Did your father *always* enjoy working?' and he wrote after finishing one big orchestral score, 'Thank God it is over and done with (all except those .... metronome-marks)' – the seven dots are Britten's own.

The satisfaction Britten felt on completing a new composition was usually short-lived. There was always a new piece to be started, and already nagging away in some corner of his mind. Though his 'fluency' may seem to be demonstrated by his large catalogue of works (at least by twentieth-century standards), this was due to his craftsman's discipline, his sheer professionalism, rather than to a simple facility. Indeed he was to say quite bluntly in 1961: 'Composition is never easy.' Yet, like Aschenbach in *Death in Venice*, he was 'driven on' by the creative process. 'Often I get exceedingly impatient if prevented from completing a work. If I have to leave Aldeburgh and an incompleted work, I am often ill because I fret so much. My state of mind is reflected in my body.' Tension, it seems, was an essential part of the Britten creative psyche. He could never have felt as did Richard Strauss, who said of his *Alpine Symphony* that he wanted 'to compose as a cow gives milk'.

A shyness as to his achievements and a reluctance to discuss his methods were lifelong Britten characteristics. When a substantial commentary on his work was published in 1952 (the symposium edited by Donald Mitchell and Hans Keller), he merely remarked, 'I've come to the conclusion that I must have a very clever subconscious.' Peter Pears has told me that he rather resented analysis as 'a kind of prying'. The pianist Graham Johnson, who knew him only in his last years, remembers him as 'very disinclined to be analytical for the purposes of savouring the triumphs of his achievements. I was intensely interested, and I think he found this rather wearing. It was as if there was a special secret about composition and creative flow which would somehow be spoiled by analysing it too much.'

Britten applied his rigorous professional standards not only in music but also in practical and administrative matters. Collaborators who could not come up to the mark found, as Graham Johnson did over some score preparation, that their services were no longer needed – though the dismissal was kindly. The composer was encouraging with amateurs, whose music-making he found 'very fresh and unstrained', but he had a sharp condemnation for 'the ineptitude of some professionals who don't know their stuff – I have no patience with that'. (He wrote: 'I have recently heard several performances of my own pieces and I felt so depressed that I considered chucking it all up! Wrong tempi, stupid phrasing and poor technique – in fact non-sense.')

Sometimes Britten turned a smouldering irritation upon his friends, and indeed upon himself. Walter Hussey recalls one such occasion during one of the earlier Aldeburgh Festivals. Auden had been there, 'rather big and overwhelming', and Britten was still recovering his composure after what had evidently been a wearing visit; for Auden had, it seems, lost none of his 'bossiness', and Britten resented this, particularly on his home ground at Aldeburgh. (Auden in turn was irritated at not being the centre of attraction, and referred rudely to 'Addleborough'.) 'We were at Crag House,' Hussey remembers. 'I went down to the festival to preach. I was preaching on the Sunday morning – Ben wasn't there – and Lord Harewood [the President of the Festival] was reading the lesson, which had been about the parable of the talents. We came back to have lunch, and there was the usual grand house party: Harewood and his wife Marion, and the French cultural attaché with his wife, and Barbara Britten. They had a long dining-room, and a huge long refectory table, quite narrow, with benches on either side. Ben was giving a recital in the afternoon, with the Amadeus Quartet: I think he was playing the Schubert 'Trout' Quintet. And Peter came in before lunch and said, "Ben won't be in to lunch, if you wouldn't mind carrying on on your own. He's just a bit worried. But if he *does* come, take no notice at all – but I'm sure he won't." So we all sat down to lunch – I think it was a cold lunch. We all were at one end of the table, so there was a huge empty space up at the other end. Peter wasn't there. And we were having a discussion on the parable of the talents: Hare-

wood was talking very intelligently. Suddenly the door opened
and in came Ben, looking like death – like he could, you know.
He looked simply awful: drawn and droopy and everything.
And he never said a word. Of course all conversation stopped
dead. Then together we all went on, as if nothing had happened.
Ben sat down, on the same side as I, but right on the far end,
leaving an enormous gap. And we went on busily discussing the
talents and almost forgot him. Then suddenly we were interrupted by a hysterical voice from the other end of the table. "It's
those who have no talents at all – they're the real problem!" And
of course we were absolutely silenced. You couldn't really say
anything. Then – fools rushing in where angels fear to tread – I
said, "meaning yourself, Ben?" And he said in the same hysterical voice: "There are times when I feel I have no talents – no
talents at all!" And so again, a great silence. Then I leant
forward and said, "You know, Ben, when you're in this sort of
mood we love you best of all." And he simply gave a great shout.
"I hate you, Walter!" From that moment, he was entirely all
right! It was very strange: a tremendous tension built up, and
then it was like lancing a boil. After that he chatted and was
friendly and went off and gave a marvellous concert.'

Britten once remarked wryly that his doctor told him he was
neurotic. According to the *Concise Oxford Dictionary* the word can
mean two things, 'affected with nervous disorder' or simply 'of
abnormal sensibility'. The latter definition sounds less unhealthy
if one substitutes the word 'exceptional' for 'abnormal'. An artist
is almost by definition exceptional: Stravinsky, in curious Ameri-
canese, once defined a genius as a 'hopeful monster' – someone
unusual but in a positive sense. Britten himself enlarged on this
theme when he received the Freedom of the Borough of Lowestoft in the summer of 1951. Speaking in his native town, he said
that while composers did not belong to a different species from
'ordinary' people, their thought and feeling had to go deeper.
'Artists are artists,' he declared, 'because they have an extra
sensitivity – a skin less, perhaps, than other people ... So ...
when you hear of an artist saying or doing something strange or
unpopular, think of that extra sensitivity – that skin less ... It
is a proud privilege to be a creative artist, but it can also be
painful.' Since his death some have argued that Britten's shyness,

his touchiness even, was mainly produced by conflicts deriving from his psychosexual nature. He himself would have hated being thought of as 'a homosexual'; but that was merely characteristic of him in the same way as he disliked being labelled as 'an opera composer' or perhaps even 'a pacifist'. Peter Pears has denied to me that Britten was burdened by a sense of guilt in the way that some (even among his admirers) might like to suppose. He was, as his sister Beth told me, quite simply 'a very private person', a non-Bohemian who believed in 'decent living', and wished neither to wave banners in the service of causes nor to indulge in *ex cathedra* pronouncements about music.

The theme of refraining from such pronouncements may seem a negative one, but it provided an interesting and revealing basis for his speech of acceptance of an Honorary Doctorate in Music at Hull University in 1962. 'I am a creative artist and therefore suffer frequently from depressions and lack of confidence,' he said, and went on: 'I admit that I hate speaking in public. It is not really a matter of natural shyness, but because I do not easily think in words, because words are not my medium. This may surprise some people, but I suppose it is the way one's brain is made. I have always found reading music easier than reading books . . . I also have a very real dread of becoming one of those artists who *talk*. I believe so strongly that it is dangerous for artists to *talk* – in public, that is; in private one really cannot stop them! – the artist's job is to *do*, not to talk about what he does. *That* is the job of other people (critics, for instance, but I'm not always so sure about this). I am all for listening to music, looking at pictures, reading novels – rather than talking about them. It is natural for composers to have strong opinions about music, and very narrow ones. They have to be selective . . . Of course I have said silly things – and these were eagerly taken up in some quarters. This sort of thing, provocative and rather scandalous, always is taken up, because it makes news . . . one particular composer I can think of, one of the greatest artistic figures of our time, has said some very misleading things, things which must have bewildered many young composers, many musical people. His judgements of other men's music often seem to me arrogant and ignorant, and they are always changing . . . how I wish he would keep quiet about them. [Presumably he was thinking of Stravinsky.] ... We should try to be obliging if we are asked to speak in public, but keep off our own personal likes and dislikes.'

With the establishment of the Aldeburgh Festival as an annual event, Britten had a place both in which and *for* which to work. Each festival had to have a new composition from its resident founder-composer. The second, in 1949, followed *Saint Nicolas* with another Britten-Crozier collaboration, *The Little Sweep*. This was a children's opera. The idea of such a piece was one that Britten had considered for a long time, perhaps ever since Aaron Copland had played him his own school piece, *The Second Hurricane*, in Snape before the war. In 1940, while in America, Britten had written in a *New York Times* article that there were 'school operas to be written, and pieces for the numberless school children learning to play instruments'. Now, having toyed with an Arthur Ransome story, he finally chose his central child character from William Blake, the sweep-boy from the *Songs of Innocence*. Crozier produced a scenario telling of the eight-year old Sammy who is rescued from a life of drudgery by the nursery-maid and three children of Iken Hall in Suffolk, and Britten wrote his score in two weeks during April 1949. One novel and successful feature was the use of the audience for four songs: novel, that is, in opera, although the same thing had occurred in *Saint Nicolas* and was later to prove effective in *Noye's Fludde*. At the first performance on 14 June 1949 in Aldeburgh's Jubilee Hall some of the audience were to raise their eyebrows at the diminished octaves (C sharp–C natural) in five-four time that feature in the opening audience number, the 'Sweep's Song'; at least the adults did, but the Ipswich schoolchildren taking part, innocent of conventional musical training, sang this new and lively music with confidence and skill.

The winter of 1948–9 had been a busy one, delaying *The Little Sweep* until the spring. Britten wrote on 5 November to John Maud: 'Peter is working in USA – but not enjoying it much, except for the work. I'm here, slaving away at new masterpieces, & enjoying it hugely. The weather couldn't be lovelier, nor the fishing more picturesque (& productive).' One 'new master-piece' was a commission from Serge Koussevitzky for a new symphonic work that had already been kept waiting for over a year ('I *must* ... think about poor old Koussevitzky's piece'), the vocal-orchestral *Spring Symphony* which was finally orchestrated by June 1949 and performed the following month in Amsterdam. (The first American performance, under Koussevitzky, was on 13 August and the English première on 9 March 1950, under Eduard van Beinum in London's Royal Albert Hall.) And now there were plans also for a big-scale new opera, commissioned for the 1951 Festival of Britain celebrations, for which E. M. Forster would provide a libretto. On 15 March 1949 Britten wrote to Jean Maud:

> Work is going magnificently here. The opera libretto with Morgan Forster is ploughing ahead, & I feel it is going to be a very big thing indeed. He is a splendid person, and enjoying working here a great deal. I have at last completed the sketches of the Spring Symphony, & am most relieved & happy about it ... We are in the midst of a whacking great financial crisis in the Group, and also I've been embroiled in a horrible British Council - Boosey & Hawkes row - but that doesn't diminish the effect of the heavenly weather today, or what fun the opera work is being, & how pleased I am to have got the old symphony polished off!

In another letter, dated 7 March, he told the Mauds:

> I heard 37 Ipswich children, possibles for the Festival children's opera, on Monday & was *enormously* impressed. It was all organised by the Co-op, & all sorts and conditions of children turned up. But the combination of skill & assurance was staggering. I feel the next generation of Britons is going to be a knock-out, in the best sense too! Most encouraging.

The Festival of Britain opera, commissioned by the Arts Council of Great Britain, was a project that had matured fairly slowly. E. M. Forster and Britten had known each other for a few years, and *Albert Herring* had been dedicated 'in admiration' to the writer; at the Aldeburgh Festival of 1948 Forster had lectured on Crabbe and speculated upon what a Peter Grimes opera 'would have been like if I had written it'. Britten remembered these words. He thought for a while of a collaboration in a comedy, and naturally enough also of a chamber opera suit-

able for the English Opera Group; but Forster had not warmed
to either of these ideas. But now the Arts Council commission
came: the new opera would have to be on a grand scale. Britten
approached Forster again and suggested using as a story Herman Melville's short novel *Billy Budd*, to which their mutual
friend William Plomer had contributed an introduction on its
reprinting in 1946. It tells of a handsome, innocent sailor in the
English navy, who unintentionally kills the malevolent master-
at-arms who has falsely accused him of mutiny and must therefore (despite his essential innocence) be hanged. The shipboard
cast for *Billy Budd* would have to be entirely male, and the hero
handicapped by the stammer that was a crucial feature of the
plot: and neither of these features seemed operatically easy.
Nevertheless there would be the spectacle and action of a war-
ship at sea with her large crew, as well as the unfolding of a
claustrophobic psychological drama. Forster was attracted by
the idea: indeed (as Britten knew) he had written twenty years
before praising Melville's story and its 'blackness and sadness so
transcending our own that they are indistinguishable from
glory'. But he was diffident about his own ability as a novice
theatrical writer, and it was quickly agreed that Eric Crozier
should also be brought in as a collaborator.

Late in 1948 Crozier was summoned to Aldeburgh, where
Britten and Forster handed him *Billy Budd* and shut him up in
a room to read right through it. As Crozier recalls: 'Their
eagerness for a favourable verdict was all too plain. As soon as
I emerged, later that morning, serious discussion began of the
great merits of the story and the problems that it presented for
stage adaptation. This went on through lunch and until tea-
time when, after a short walk, we settled round the fire with
Melville's book and a notepad. My first "manuscript" includes
two short lists in Britten's writing, one recording all the characters that Melville names, the second listing the dramatic epi-
sodes as they occur in the book. There is also a third sheet, which
consists of a sketchy side-view of a sailing-ship, drawn by Britten,
slightly modified by me, and annotated by Forster with place-
names – Main Deck, Quarter Deck, Captain's Cabin – to help
us find our way around.' This was the first of five manuscripts,
the last of which, much later, was to be the final libretto of 1951.

(Though ten years later the work was to be revised and compressed from the original four acts into two.) In March 1949 Forster and Crozier were working together at Britten's house; 'Britten was busy scoring his Spring Symphony, but midway through the morning he would visit us to see how things were going. We met at meals and talked about *Billy*: we went for walks and talked about *Billy*: friends came in the evenings and for politeness' sake we talked about other things, but our minds were still on *Billy*.' Having drafted the main scenes, they left their typescript with the composer, returning at his invitation in August to spend another month with him: 'From now on, he assumed the dominance in our partnership and led the discussions.' It was only after a revised text was written, incorporating Britten's story-line ideas, that the composer actually started to work on the music. With this libretto, as with others, he was involved from the beginning: in the choice of story, the design of the stage and the dramatic shape. As he said himself, 'I have to be in on it from the beginning.' His talent was both dramatic and musical. Indeed as a child of six or seven he had written (and probably acted in) a play called *The Royal Falily* (*sic!*), illustrated and with details of costume design as well as a tiny fragment of incidental music. Though he never claimed to create operas single-handed as Wagner did, they were 'his' own creations to an extent far greater than were those of, say, Handel or Gluck.

Billy Budd was thus 'on the stocks' for something like three years. During this gestation period other things went on, even besides those already mentioned. Britten's new version of *The Beggar's Opera*, composed for the chamber resources of the English Opera Group, was given at Aldeburgh during the 1950 festival. The group itself, as it happened, was to diminish in importance as the Aldeburgh Festival and other things (such as *Billy Budd* and *Gloriana*, operas quite unsuited to its aims and resources) preoccupied Britten. While its intention to involve other composers besides Britten himself was partially carried through with Brian Easdale's *The Sleeping Children* in 1951 and Arthur Oldham's new version of Arne's *Love in a Village* that was given at Aldeburgh the following year, there were financial problems that could not be wholly overcome, although the group survived to present Britten's *The Turn of the Screw* and

A Midsummer Night's Dream and eventually become the English Music Theatre in 1975; they were also to present, at Aldeburgh, new operas by Berkeley (three), Walton, Malcolm Williamson, Harrison Birtwistle and Gordon Crosse, as well as operas by Purcell, Monteverdi, Blow, Holst, Mozart, Gluck and Handel. Britten himself wrote some other shorter pieces in 1949–51: a 'Wedding Anthem' for his friends Marion Stein (the daughter of Erwin Stein) and George Harwood, who were married in September 1949, *Five Flower Songs* for the twenty-fifth wedding anniversary of other friends, the Elmhirsts of Darlington Hall, in April 1950, the 'Lachrymae' for viola with piano and the 'Six Metamorphoses after Ovid' for oboe solo.

Britten and Peter Pears also travelled in the autumn of 1949 to America for a recital tour. Writing on 7 March to Sir John Maud, who was about to travel there, he explained that he had already been touring in Europe and had returned depressed:

> I really am much better at last. I occasionally go right down to the bottom of the pit again; but now, happily, only for the shortest of visits. Venice was a terrific success & we even had warm sun. Perhaps it was a bit too much of a success since when I got back I found I wasn't quite so much better as I'd thought I was. But I'm now starting work again ... You might, if the chance permits, mention that two frightened mice you know are coming over in the Fall, & please be nice to them? I couldn't be more worried about anything, nor yet (frankly) more bored about going. I don't know why one does it – one can't pretend that the few dollars we'll earn can make much difference to the dollar rate.

He and Pears sailed from Southampton after the Harewood wedding at the end of September, and gave a coast-to-coast tour including a New York Town Hall concert on 23 October. In Hollywood he saw *Albert Herring* in rehearsal in a production by Carl Ebert for the University of Southern California. With Pears, he also visited Stravinsky in his Hollywood home on 24 November; six days later the great Russian attended a Britten concert at the university and early in December Stravinsky went to see *Herring*. Britten's admiration for Stravinsky was great but not unqualified, and seems to have been reciprocated similarly;

one would love to know how the conversation went when they met, but the senior composer's brilliant Boswell, Robert Craft, was unfortunately not present.

The main work upon *Billy Budd* was done between February 1950 and the autumn of 1951. But Britten wanted, somehow or other, also to provide the English Opera Group with a new opera for their 1951 season, fearing that the group should feel neglected in the important Festival of Britain year, and he did so by enlisting the services of two collaborators (as it were), Henry Purcell and Imogen Holst. Purcell's *Dido and Aeneas* was an opera he loved and, with Imogen Holst as joint editor and amanuensis, he made a 'realisation' from the best available manuscript, the one found in the library of St Michael's College, Tenbury. It was the same kind of work as he had done with Purcell's songs and the original airs of *The Beggar's Opera*; for the missing chorus at the end of Act II (where text and the indication of a dance, but no music, exists) Britten borrowed other Purcell music – and incidentally in the process made the Act end in the correct key, that with which it began. Scored for strings with harpsichord continuo, the new version of *Dido and Aeneas* was given its first performance by the English Opera Group at the Lyric Theatre, Hammersmith, on 1 May 1951. Nancy Evans played Dido, Joan Cross produced and Britten himself directed from the keyboard. The production then went to Aldeburgh for the 1951 festival, to Cheltenham and Liverpool, and also to Holland, a country where Britten was greatly valued, and where the composer and critic Marius Flothuis referred in 1949 to his 'amazing talent and tremendous productive capacity ... some even regard him as having genius'.

In the summer of 1951 Britten was given the Freedom of the Borough of Lowestoft. The ceremony took place on 28 July in the Sparrow's Nest Theatre. It was no empty honour to the composer, who was touched by this gesture from the people of his birthplace. In his speech of acceptance (already quoted) he recalled an earlier appearance in that theatre when aged about three, playing Tom the water-baby – significantly an *escaped sweep-boy* in Charles Kingsley's tale – 'dressed in skin-coloured tights, with madly curly hair, trying desperately to remember the lines'. Rather more seriously, he explained something of his creed regarding his calling. 'As an artist, I want to serve the community. In other days, artists were the servants of institutions like the Church, or of private patrons. Today it is the community that orders the artist about. It is not a bad thing to try to serve all sorts of different people and to have to work to order. Any artist worth his salt has ... ideas knocking about in his head, and an invitation to write something can often direct these ideas into a concrete form and shape. Of course, it can sometimes be difficult when one doesn't feel in the mood, but perhaps that's good for one, too! – anyhow, composers (like other people) can be horribly lazy, and often this is the only way that they can be made to produce something!'

Sixteen years later, interviewed for a television documentary, Britten was to talk further about his work. 'The feeling is that the creator, the artist, has a moment of sudden inspiration, and dashes to the paper or canvas and, in the height of inspiration writes down or paints this wonderful picture that is in his mind. In my experience, that isn't the way that I work. I like working to an exact timetable. I often thank my stars that I had a rather conventional upbringing, that I went to a rather strict school where one was made to work. And I can without much difficulty sit down at nine o'clock in the morning and work straight through the morning until lunchtime. I don't say I always enjoy the work at that time, but it isn't a great struggle to do so each day. I find, actually, that the day divides up quite naturally into three or four periods: the morning, when as I've said, I work till lunchtime, then in the afternoon letters – or, rather more important, is that I go for a walk, where I plan out what I'm going to write in the next period at my desk. I then come back. After tea, up to my studio and work through until about eight o'clock. After dinner I usually find I'm too sleepy to do much more than to read a little bit, and then go to bed rather early.'

Lunchtime, tea, dinner ... these familiar landmarks in a working day are always taken for granted. Yet they are difficult without family life, the quiet routine of a household in which the breadwinner works while others shop and cook and clean and wash clothes. Britten was not one who could work, say as Beethoven had done, in bachelor Bohemianism surrounded by dirty crockery, eating out and irregularly, going at night to an unmade bed. On the other hand he was not especially efficient himself at cooking or bed-making, as Peter Pears recalls. 'Ben was not a well-trained domestic animal, I think. He could boil an egg ... but that was about as far as he'd go. He could have watched a piece of toast, I suppose, being burnt slowly. If he made his bed he made a mess of it; I mean, he did frequently make his bed, but it wasn't very comfortably made and somebody would probably have to come along and make it again for him afterwards. He liked a family life ... a regular household life, to run on fairly sure rails. Ben was never a Bohemian, in any sense of the word. He really was a working musician – a working composer.' Who, then, one asks, did the shopping and laundry and innumerable other mundane but necessary items of household routine? The answer lay in the person of Miss Hudson, Britten and Pear's housekeeper for some 25 years, who retired in 1973 to live in the Red House grounds in a cottage that they built for her. Britten liked her style of home cooking, 'nursery food' as Pears would say – a milk pudding, or a 'spotted dog', or 'dark treacle jelly'. 'But Mr Britten had to be careful,' Miss Hudson remembers, 'because he hadn't got a strong inside like Mr Pears had.' She knew how to produce appetising food, even for visitors at unexpected hours, and would serve home-bottled wine with it. She too was the one to see the two musicians off on a tour ('Have you got your passport, your money, all the music?') and then welcome them home again to a warm home.

In late September 1951 Britten and Pears went on a short holiday by motor launch with a fisherman friend called Bill Burrell and Burrell's brother; they crossed the North Sea and joined the Rhine in one of its two branches near Rotterdam and then travelled up river as far as Bonn. Returning to England, they settled down to a stage 'sea' and the *Billy Budd* rehearsals. The producer was Basil Coleman, and Britten himself was called in to conduct after the original conductor, Josef Krips, withdrew from the production. The Administrator of Covent Garden, David Webster, had auditioned in America and found Theodor Uppman, a young baritone who not only sang well but also strikingly looked the part of the handsome Billy. Peter Pears played Captain Vere, and at forty-one could play him also as an older man, as he appears in the Prologue and Epilogue. The designer was John Piper, who had the task of making a stage look like a ship, on and below decks: arches in balsa wood skilfully suggested the ship's ribs. As Coleman recalls, Britten 'was remarkable to work with', patient and encouraging with singers who found the idiom of the music hard: 'gradually the cast responded to the words and music and became more and more involved in the moving story'. The Covent Garden première was on 1 December 1951. The composer himself was pleased, and though he later revised the score *Budd* was an opera that was to remain especially dear to him. However, Peter Pears remembers that 'the press reaction to those first performances was really somewhat unsympathetic. Ben of course did mind, in the sense that to see one's own children spat at in public is a disagreeable experience. But it didn't last too long. He expected it, after a time. *Lucretia* had some extraordinarily nasty notices; *Grimes* had two very bad notices: they couldn't deny that it made them sit up and it was something lively and new, but the press all along ... I mean, who trusts the press? His opinion of critics was very, very low.' As far as *Billy Budd* was concerned, the critics used adjectives like 'flawed' and 'purposeless'.

Why was *Billy Budd* disliked, one may wonder, since today it is perhaps the most performed of Britten's operas after *Peter Grimes*? There were several reasons, all of which were predictable. Its all-male cast was hardly in tune with the conventional opera-going taste that enjoyed tenor/soprano love duets. The salt-sea orchestration, in which the first trumpet plays more notes than the first violins, was not comforting to the ear. The hint of the crucifixion with which the scene of Billy's hanging was presented upset some religious sensibilities. And of course the homosexual undertones of Melville's story, noted by Auden and others long before Britten's opera, were discussed (though not in print) and resented. (Billy's looks are mentioned more often than his virtue, while his friend Dansker even calls him 'Beauty'.) As for the evil Claggart, his hate for Billy is arguably a perversion of sexual attraction. Captain Vere, too, is more drawn towards Billy than he can admit, even to himself: in 1797 Vere cannot possess the post-Freudian self-awareness of Aschenbach in *Death in Venice*. There was more than this; for Britten's collaborator E. M. Forster was suspected of being homosexual. *Billy Budd* was referred to by some as 'The Bugger's Opera', and the *mot* was apt and funny enough, it seems, to gain currency. (Even Britten's former teacher, John Ireland, was heard to use it.)

But there were happier things too, connected with *Billy Budd*. Calling on Britten in his dressing room after he had conducted a Covent Garden performance, I found the barefoot composer both touched and amused that Edgar Evans, the Welsh tenor who doubled for Pears as Vere, had been moved to tears by the harrowing story and then found it difficult to sing. Peter Pears himself recalled an occasion when something went wrong with the gauze curtain representing the mist falling between the *Indomitable* and the French ship she intends to engage and he had to begin the original Act III (now Act II) with the line, 'I don't like the look of the mist, Mr Redburn.' And a German production of the opera, in March 1952 at Wiesbaden, was so successful that the Earl of Harewood, who attended, noted an enthusiasm he could not 'remember ever having seen exceeded elsewhere'.

In any case, Britten was by this time already thinking about a new opera. In March 1952 he was with his friends George and Marion Harewood on a skiing holiday in Austria; the King had died the previous month and Lord Harewood, the new Queen's cousin as well as an opera lover, was quick to see the possibility of a new Britten opera commission to mark the forthcoming coronation and the dawn of a new Elizabethan age. Back in London, the commission received Palace approval. As for the subject, the composer who had in childhood written a play about the royal family quickly settled on a fairly obvious choice of story, that of the first Queen Elizabeth and the Earl of Essex, as treated by Lytton Strachey in 1928. As librettist he chose his friend, the poet and novelist William Plomer, who had known Strachey at that time. Joan Cross was asked to play the Queen and Peter Pears Essex; while John Pritchard was chosen to conduct, John Piper to design and Basil Coleman to produce. The date of the première, 8 June 1953, was announced at the end of May. For a title, he and Plomer chose an old name for Elizabeth I, *Gloriana*. The composer was delighted with his new librettist, finding him 'fine to work with: reasonable and skilful ... a treasure'. The music had to be written in between other work during 1952: there was, as always, the Aldeburgh Festival, as well as concerts in Denmark, France and Austria. He really settled down to the opera in the autumn, working about an eight-hour day with a game of tennis or a swim during his 'hours off' in the afternoon, or perhaps a long walk over the marshes. He kept to his carefully planned schedule, finishing the sketch just after the New Year, and then scored the whole work at the rate of twenty or more pages (of 34-stave paper) each day, aided in such matters as writing clefs and drawing bar-lines by his assistant from September 1952, Imogen Holst.

As William Plomer was later to write, *Gloriana* is 'less concerned than Strachey with the amatory motive of the two principal characters and more concerned with the Queen's pre-eminence as a Queen, a woman and a personality'. Basil Coleman, as producer, had to bear in mind the striking contrast between 'the Queen as she presented herself in public, then revealed herself in private; between the lonely woman's longing for a close human relationship and her fear of its possible consequences for her people and her country; between her sense of her own power and her humility before God'. It is possible even to see a parallel between her situation (as Queen, she must sign Essex's death-warrant) and that of Captain Vere in *Billy Budd*. *Gloriana* is like *Budd*, too, in offering both grand spectacle and intimate psychological drama: what Erwin Stein wrote of the earlier opera applies here also, that 'none of its spectacular features has been abandoned, but operatic expression has been given wider scope.' Thus there was the pageantry – the masque at Norwich, the dancing in the Palace of Whitehall – and the beautiful sets and costumes that were to earn an ovation for John Piper; but there were intimate scenes too, especially between the Queen and Essex but not exclusively between these two principals.

Gloriana was dedicated 'by gracious permission' to the young Queen Elizabeth II. Before the Royal Gala première at Covent Garden on 8 June 1953, honouring the coronation, the composer and librettist, Plomer later wrote,

had a long evening in private with the Queen and Prince Philip to tell them what they were in for. They couldn't have been more amiable, and although neither is musical, both paid close attention. Prince Philip is quite as Germanically thorough as the Prince Consort, but has a more practical and varied experience of life, is versatile, and has a much lighter touch and a sense of fun.

It seems that the royal couple were amused to learn that a street scene in which a slattern empties a chamberpot from her window over the rabble-rouser Cuffe had had to be changed; a basin was substituted because 'the Lord Chamberlain has had *to set his face against chamber-pots*'.

So far, so good. Nevertheless the première of *Gloriana* was not a success. The production was a fine one and the sets and costumes splendid, and though the conductor John Pritchard could not attend the first rehearsals, the musical side was well managed and, according to Basil Coleman, Joan Cross as the Queen gave 'a great performance'. Yet William Plomer was later to write that the opera 'had a curiously mixed reception'; indeed in private he went further and called it 'hostile'. (Woodrow Wyatt, in a letter to *The Times* some days later, used the word 'frigid', reproaching the audience.) At the final curtain the composer and librettist heard 'no more than a cold sprinkling of applause' and Britten leaned over from their box above the stalls muttering 'Clap, damn you, clap!' Was it the wholly muted ending, with the dying Queen alone on stage, that left the audience puzzled and reserved? Some things in the opera were not to all tastes: there was a striking but controversial moment at the start of Act III when Essex bursts in upon the Queen to find her without her wig and bald, a pathetic ageing figure. The audience itself consisted of heads of state, politicians and diplomats, really little more than the international equivalent of a borough mayor and councillors and with no special musical inclination. In the foyer before the performance, indeed, someone was heard to say that the new opera was 'by this Benjamin Bradford, about Queen Elizabeth and Lord Darnley'. 'Alas, the ears of the mighty are often mighty long ears,' Plomer quoted bitterly from Voltaire.

Some music critics at the *Gloriana* première seem to have taken their own cue from the cool reaction of an unmusical audience, and there were unfavourable reviews to which Britten's reaction was abrupt, and typical – 'if I had listened to the critics I would have given up writing music long ago'. A critic's comment on his colleagues was made by Martin Cooper, who wrote in the *Spectator* that 'the work has been very generally overblamed, with an almost sadistic relish or glee that has little to do with musical merit or demerit'. But there was a reaction. Vaughan Williams declared that the Sovereign's commission was a matter for pride, while correspondents to *The Times* and *Observer* wrote of 'superb richness and invention' and 'a variety of musical splendours', and the *New Statesman* hailed a work 'which gleams with intelligence and charm and skill'. The *Manchester Guardian* critic noted 'the clear demonstration, clearer even than in Britten's previous operas, of the Verdian quality, in the sense both of kind and of power, of his genius'.

Subsequent Covent Garden audiences liked *Gloriana* well enough; and so did audiences outside London when the opera was toured. And with a new Sadler's Wells production in August 1966 it was to become established as a repertory piece. William Plomer, however, on that much later occasion had to be more or less dragged on to the stage by Britten to share in their curtain calls: 'I was thinking of the long delay in the recognition of *Gloriana*, and kept a grave face.'

8

West meets east (1954–63)

Death in Venice, Act I

Gloriana marked a milestone in Britten's career. He was created a Companion of Honour on 1 June 1953, a week before the première, so joining an exclusive order of distinguished persons limited to sixty-five members; at thirty-nine, he was exceptionally young to be so honoured. (Twelve years later he was to receive the Order of Merit, limited to twenty-four members; and in the year of his death he was created a life peer, an honour never before accorded to a composer.) But it was characteristic of him to accept honours that enhanced the status of his art and profession while not using these as an excuse to rest, even briefly, on his acquired laurels. Thus even while working on *Gloriana* he was already thinking about his next opera, a work commissioned for performance by the English Opera Group at the Biennale Festival in Venice during 1954. Since this was to be a chamber opera (having the same relationship to 'grand' opera, Britten once said, as a string quartet to a symphony) the subject had to be more intimate than that of *Gloriana*. The idea of using Henry James's famous ghost story, *The Turn of the Screw*, came from Myfanwy Piper who, as John Piper's wife, had been familiar with all Britten's operas from *Lucretia* onwards. Britten decided to ask her to write the libretto, although she lived in Oxfordshire, a long way from Aldeburgh, and the kind of close, prolonged collaboration that he liked would not be possible. 'Goodness,' he wrote to Basil Coleman, who was to produce, '– how difficult it is to write an opera with the librettist so far away. She is so good, but is so occupied with being a wife and mother! ... I have never felt so insecure about a work – now up, now down – and it helps a great deal to know that you, who know so instinctively what I'm aiming at, like it so much.'

In the late summer of 1953, before starting work on the new opera, Britten wrote a new song cycle, *Winter Words*, to eight Thomas Hardy poems. This was performed by Peter Pears and himself on 8 October at Harewood House near Leeds, as part of the Leeds Triennial Festival. The cycle possesses a rich humanity and warmth, and a response too to natural beauty, though it ends with the intensely serious song 'Before Life and After'. It was dedicated to John and Myfanwy Piper and seemed a fitting compliment to *The Turn of the Screw*'s future designer and librettist. Then, quite unexpectedly, Britten's schedule was interrupted when he fell ill with acute bursitis, an inflammation of the bursal sac in his right shoulder. He had to cancel all conducting and recital work, drive a left-hand-drive Mercedes and do his best to write with his left hand. A typed letter to the Mauds, dated 3 December, explained the situation:

> Actually having swapped around from doctor to doctor, I'm, as it were, nicely suited now with a good g.p. and first-class specialist, who are doing all they can with this most obscure trouble. Actually the most important thing seems to be rest, and to that end I'm soon off abroad for some weeks. But it is the most awful bore – although I'm getting on well with my left-handed music writing.

A week later he thanked me for birthday greetings on 22 November in a typed postcard with a spidery signature; this was unexplained until a further letter in March which showed a sense of urgency about the forthcoming opera: 'Owing to a maddeningly protracted arm infection capped by a visit to hospital last week I am extremely behind hand with my work, and must stay rigorously in Aldeburgh for the next two or three months.' What had caused the bursitis no one knew for certain, but Britten's remark earlier that year about conducting ('I'm too tense nearly all the time') provides a possible clue.

The Turn of the Screw, set in an English country house in the middle of the last century, tells of two young children, Miles and Flora, and the ghosts of Peter Quint and Miss Jessel who strive to possess them; the heroine is the young governess who realises the situation and resolves to save her beloved charges. Britten and Myfanwy Piper decided on two acts, each broken up into eight scenes but without a pause in the music, which in fact is a theme and fifteen variations. The scene at the start of Act II, in which the ghosts are seen and heard in dialogue, was Britten's suggestion: a passage in which these former lovers bitterly evoke their past. Otherwise the libretto is close to the original story; though by making the ghosts appear, and indeed sing, Britten and Mrs Piper settled the question of the ghosts' 'reality' and removed the possibility, left just open by James, that the governess has imagined them. Britten started composing the music in March 1954, immediately after his return from hospital. He wrote to reassure his collaborator:

> I started the opera this morning and have quite good progress to report. I have got well into the first scene – I am quite pleased with it ... The best plan seems to be for me to go on working and writing the suggestions of changes daily (or telephoning if they are urgent) and when it seems to need your actual presence I will write to you suggesting it and hope you may be able to fit it in ... Thank you for your suggestions of titles ... I must confess that I have a sneaking horrid feeling that the original H.J. title describes the musical plan of the work *exactly*!!

In fact the opera was written fairly quickly; one of its most complex sections, the brisk thirteen-part fugue in five-four time (Act I, Variation 5) was composed on the train between Ipswich and Liverpool Street. The Venice festival fee was substantial enough to cover a month of rehearsals, and a strong cast was assembled, with Jennifer Vyvyan as the Governess, Joan Cross as the housekeeper Mrs Grose, and Peter Pears and Arda Mandikian as the ghosts. The twelve-year-old David Hemmings (later to become a well-known film actor) was chosen for the important part of Miles, but for musical safety's sake a slightly-built adult singer, Olive Dyer, was cast as Flora. The final week of rehearsals took place in Venice. The première itself, in the Teatro la Fenice on 14 September, was preceded by the usual first-night nerves, not least on the part of the composer; but it went well and there was a happy feeling of a gala occasion, with roses placed in each box that filled the theatre (itself small and lovely) with a scent quite appropriate for the English country-house setting of the opera. As well as the individual perform-ances, the ensemble of the whole production was praised by the public and press alike, and for once the composer was in high spirits about the reception of his new work. Eventually he trav-elled back to England with Pears, Basil Coleman and Imogen Holst in his open car, Pears and he taking it in turns to drive – a perfect 'unwinding' after the various strains and excitements. *The Turn of the Screw* was heard the following month at Sadler's Wells in London. On 12 October Britten wrote to Jean Maud: 'I am so glad you liked "The Screw" – we are excited by the way the audience rises to it.'

A few weeks after this Britten and Pears drove down to Lanc-ing, in Sussex, and spent a quiet weekend with their old friend Mrs Esther Neville-Smith. I was at this time in my first term as a Lancing College music master, a post Britten had encouraged me to take, and was a lodger in the same attractive old house, Friar's Acre, in North Lancing village. There were delicious meals and happy, relaxed conversation afterwards, by no means always about music. William Plomer came over from his Rus-tington home and Britten drove him back there in Peter Pears's Morris late one evening; I went along 'for the ride' in the back seat. Returning to Lancing, and garaging the car, he said that he thought *The Turn of the Screw* the best thing he had done so far but added that writing it had been hard, like 'finding things for people to do in a house party' and sometimes like 'squeezing toothpaste out of a tube that's nearly finished' – remarks which presumably have to do with the opera's very tight organisation and its exceptional economy of musical means.

Pears and Britten returned Mrs Neville-Smith's hospitality that Christmas. She wrote to me from 4 Crabbe Street on 28 December:

We all send you most appreciative thanks for your superb box of luscious crystallised fruit, which we have been consuming steadily. It would have pleased you to have seen Peter and Mary Potter choosing their favourite kinds at a Christmas gathering here last night. Such a lovely time! now coming to an end. Arda Mandikian has been staying here too, and Imogen Holst is in and out, and there is sunshine and music and the most poetic food! Peter and Ben say kind things about you …

(They added after her signature 'Lovely glacé fruits!! Peter P.' and '& love from Ben too!')

Early in 1955 there were recitals with Peter Pears in Belgium and Switzerland, followed by another skiing holiday at Zermatt. Britten's painter friend Mary Potter, who was there, hurt her leg and he at once composed an 'Alpine Suite' for recorder trio which the two of them and Peter Pears played in the evenings. Soon after this he wrote a Scherzo for recorder quartet for the Aldeburgh Music Club, with whom he occasionally liked to play. Some of 1955 was spent with the English Opera Group, touring in Germany and Italy with *The Turn of the Screw*, and then with the festival at Aldeburgh. He also conducted recordings of the *Screw*, *Saint Nicolas* and *The Little Sweep*. For once he was doing little in the way of composition. But he was planning: a year before he had agreed to compose something quite new for him, a full-length ballet to be given at Covent Garden by the Sadler's Wells Theatre Ballet with choreography by John Cranko. (A number of ballets had used Britten's music, but this was the first piece that he planned especially for this purpose.) Cranko's draft scenario for *The Prince of the Pagodas* was ready in plenty of time and Britten gave it thought throughout 1955 without writing any of the music. Instead he went, for the first time in his life, to Asia and returned in March 1956 with his head full of ideas that were to take an early shape in the ballet music and indeed to influence much of his subsequent work.

The five-month concert tour that was to take Britten and Pears to Asia started in November 1955. They went first to Austria, Yugoslavia and Turkey, and then travelled to Singapore. There, on 6 January 1956, they were joined by Prince

Ludwig of Hesse and his British-born wife Peg: these were friends met through the Harewoods in 1952, who were now close and congenial. Prince Ludwig kept a diary, privately printed as *Ausflug Ost* ('Eastern Excursion'), which records their experiences over the ten weeks or so that ended with a return to Europe on 16 March. Pears and Britten performed Schubert's *Die schöne Müllerin* on 6 January in Singapore and gave further recitals in Indonesia (Djakarta and Bandung); in Bandung the composer also enjoyed the sound of a children's orchestra of percussion instruments, zithers and flutes, and he pleased the young performers by singing through the basic scale of their music. In Semarang there was a visit to a gong factory and in Surabaja another concert. Then on 12 January they flew to Denpasar in Bali – one of the most beautiful places in the world – and Britten fell in love with the island. The day after their arrival they bathed and walked along the beach, and in the evening listened to young men in sarongs playing 'tropical serenades' with titles like *A Frog Climbs a Banana Tree and then Falls Out Again*. The Balinese *gamelan* orchestra of metallophones (tuned percussion), gongs and drums was a memorable experience with its 'liquid, bronze sound'. The composer wrote to Imogen Holst that this was a place where the music was part of the atmosphere, like 'the palm trees, the spicy smells, and the charming beautiful people. ... *fantastically* rich – melodically, rhythmically, texture (such *orchestration*!) and above all *formally* ... At last I'm beginning to catch on to the technique.' In Bali there was plenty of palm wine to drink but also some alarmingly primitive lavatories, one of which reminded the composer of a 'late work of his friend Henry Moore'. In such a hot climate bathing was a necessary pleasure, and on one occasion a sudden refreshing rainstorm just after bedtime took the composer, together with the Prince and his brother-in-law John Geddes, out into the garden for a birthday-suited shower. The travellers were also persuaded to dress up in native costume to be photographed and amused to look altogether ridiculous: according to the Princess, Peter Pears 'looked like a Rhine Maiden', while 'Ben also togged up looked like a governess at a fancy dress'.

   Leaving Bali on 25 January 1956 for Surabaja and Surakarta, the concert tour recommenced. Britten's 'tummy', never the most reliable of organs, gave occasional trouble but was to some extent calmed by supplies of brandy and abstinence from sea-food. On 2 February they arrived in Hong Kong. Pears and Britten performed the following evening before the Governor and an audience of 1300; they gave another recital the day after in the tiny Portuguese territory of Macau. On 8 February they flew to Tokyo. There on 18 February Britten was to conduct a concert for NHK, the Japanese Radio, including the *Sinfonia da Requiem* (written sixteen years before in response to a Jap-anese commission), *Les Illuminations* and *The Young Person's Guide to the Orchestra*; Pears sang in the orchestral cycle and also did the narration in the Guide. The composer's less formal Japanese musical experience included joining in madrigals and even accompanying a lady hostess in a song by one of his less favourite composers, Brahms, after which he organised some rounds for everyone to sing.

But the most important musical and dramatic experience of the twelve days in Japan was one in which Britten was a spec-tator rather than a participant. This was an afternoon perform-ance in Tokyo on 11 February 1956 of the classical *Nō* drama *Sumidagawa* ('Sumida River'), written in the fifteenth century by Jūrō Motomasa. This story of a madwoman (played by a male actor) seeking her lost child was presented in a highly stylised, even hieratic manner, and even though the initial impression was of 'deadly serious gibberish', it made a deep impression on Britten. He was later to write that 'the solemn dedication and skill of the performers were a lesson to any singer or actor of any country and any language'. It was William Plomer (who had lived in Japan) who had recommended him to see a *Nō* play; later he and the poet used this same story for the 'church parable' *Curlew River*. The 'totally new "operatic" experience', as Britten called it, was thus to make a clear mark in his music following the Asian journey, as did the evocative and seductive sound of the Balinese *gamelan* which re-emerged almost at once with his ballet music for *The Prince of the Pagodas*. In the meantime the pagodas of Bangkok marked the first stage in a slow return to England via Singapore (where he and Pears performed Schubert and the *Michelangelo Sonnets* in the choir of an Anglican cathedral of 'candied Gothic'), Ceylon and India (more music –

the tambura or drone lute, flute and drums); mild Madras curry, strong cool whisky and friendly British Council officials made this an agreeable end to a memorable working holiday. Finally, when 'British Overdue Airways' failed to arrive at Karachi, a Pan American aircraft carried the much-travelled quartet back to Frankfurt, and after a night at Schloss Wolfsgarten, the Hesses' home, the two English musicians set off for Aldeburgh.

Britten composed the ballet, *The Prince of the Pagodas* in the autumn of 1956, and it proved to be hard work. Over two hours of orchestral music was a major undertaking, and of course it was the longest purely instrumental piece he had ever written. He studied the Tchaikovsky ballets, considering these the best models for an extended balletic work. As for formal structure, something not considered by any textbook, he had to find a way of holding the music together so that it would be more than a mere incidental commentary on the stage action. The formal problems were akin to (but not identical with) those of opera. In the words of Erwin Stein: 'It is not only a question of inventing many good and diverse tunes, but also of co-ordinating and balancing them. And as rhythm is the life blood of dancing, it is especially the rhythmic shapes of the tunes that must be well defined and diversified.' One notices Stein's emphasis on the idea of 'tunes': in a work such as this, simplicity and broad effects had to be the keynote. Nevertheless the deliciously *frisson*-filled music for the pagoda-land scene, as close to *gamelan* music as the western instruments permitted, was subtle enough for any connoisseur. If the *Pagodas* were an offshoot of the Asian trip, so were the *Songs from the Chinese* of 1957, written for Pears and the guitarist Julian Bream and dedicated 'to Peg and Lu', in other words the Hesses.

The Prince of the Pagodas was Britten's only major composition in 1956; apart from this there was just a short Antiphon for choir and organ written for the centenary of St Michael's College, Tenbury. He did manage to enjoy further holidays that summer, however, partly with the Hesses at Schloss Tarasp, their castle in the eastern corner of Switzerland, beautifully situated high up in the Engadine. Peter Pears was there too, and the foursome also visited Siena and Venice. The two musicians made a trip to Cannes to renew an old friendship with the composer Francis

Poulenc. In November 1956 they were abroad again, this time giving recitals in Germany. The enormous job of scoring the 125-minute *Pagodas* music kept Britten busy, indeed under especial pressure during that autumn. For once he had under-estimated the magnitude of the task; the original date for the première of the ballet (19 September) had had to be postponed.

In fact *The Prince of the Pagodas* received its first performance on New Year's Day, 1957. The Sadler's Wells production at Covent Garden, in which Svetlana Beriosova and David Blair danced the main roles, was something of a gala occasion. Britten conducted and at the end was presented with a giant laurel wreath. The Royal Ballet took the work to New York some months later, and it was also mounted at La Scala, Milan. And there was a recording in London in February, in which the composer conducted the Covent Garden Orchestra. As for criti-cal reaction, Donald Mitchell wrote of the ballet: 'Throughout the piece Britten's genius burns at its very brightest ... it might be said that the *Pagodas* combines the loose build and, on occa-sions, festal atmosphere of *Gloriana* with the concentrated, total thematic organisation of *The Turn of the Screw*.'

Nevertheless Britten felt tired and worn at the beginning of 1957. He wrote from Aldeburgh to Jean Maud on 31 January:

How nice of you to write so warmly. I am awfully pleased you enjoyed the 'Pagodas'. It's being nice & successful, so they are going to play it on & off throughout the Spring, I gather. Yes – I'm laid up here for a week or so now, & then back to London for the pretty arduous task of recording all the music from the Ballet! I shall be around in London for several weeks, & much hope there'll be a chance of seeing you all. I'm feeling pretty low still, but starting to come up from the bottom of the pit ... it's pretty depressing down there!

In fact there were no new Britten compositions until the autumn of 1957. But in the meantime he was elected an honorary member of the American Academy of Arts and Letters in April; the American ambassador in London read a citation stating that his works did honour both to himself and to England. In the same month he completed a recording in London in which he conducted two vocal works, *A Boy was Born* and *Rejoice in the Lamb*. The early summer brought the busy festival time at Aldeburgh, where the English Opera Group presented Lennox Berkeley's *Ruth*, to a libretto by Eric Crozier on the biblical story. After that Britten sailed in August to Canada with the group, where in Stratford, Ontario, he directed performances of *The Turn of the Screw*. In October he was in Berlin for more performances of the same opera.

Back in Aldeburgh, two things awaited Britten urgently: the move to a new house and the composition of a new opera. In November he moved to The Red House, near Aldeburgh's golf course, exchanging houses with his painter friend Mary Potter. Being a couple of miles inland he lost the sea view from his studio, but he became less accessible to the view of a curious public. The house was also comfortably large with a tennis court and a vegetable garden; and though there was no immediate sea bathing he could now enjoy the luxury of his own small pool. As for the operatic project, Eric Crozier had had an idea for a new children's opera; or at least it was he who presented the composer with a copy of the Chester Miracle Play *Noye's Fludde*, a sixteenth-century text giving a colourful account of the biblical 'flood' story with more than a sprinkling of humour in the persons of the formidable Mrs Noye and her bibulous friends. The young English Opera Group producer Colin Graham was given charge of the new work, which was discussed during the Canadian tour. Britten started work on the music on 22 October at 4 Crabbe Street and finished it two months later at his new home.

The first performance of *Noye's Fludde* was scheduled to take place during the 1958 Aldeburgh Festival, in Orford Church on 18 June; the choice of a church rather than a theatre (if the Jubilee Hall could be so called) was of course deliberate in view of the Miracle Plays' original association with the church. Britten wanted to use amateur performers as far as possible, following medieval precedent; thus there were a few necessary professionals (for example Noye and Mrs Noye, and the orchestral timpanist) but was mainly made up of children both on 'stage' and in the orchestra, which was visible to the side of the action, playing recorders, strings, handbells, bugles and percussion. Drawing as far as possible on existing local skills, Britten wrote the handbell parts for the children of Leiston Modern School and the bugles' music for young players from the Royal Hospital School, Holbrook. The percussion group from Woolverstone Hall had a special instrument invented for them, a series of mugs strung up on a string which gave vaguely different notes when struck with a wooden spoon and which were to suggest memorably the first raindrops on the roof of the Ark. The large number of children who dressed up as animals – 'camelles', 'doggës' and squeaking mice – came from various East Suffolk schools. This Aldeburgh Festival event was in no way a sophisticated and expensive occasion for leisured visitors from London or further afield; it was a local production by local people.

Yet *Noye's Fludde*, perhaps because of its deep human roots, has a universality that has struck many a performer or listener – and in any case the congregation listeners also participate in three hymns and so also 'perform'. It is a Britten work that has proved accessible to virtually any English community and as such has been given over and over again, becoming an institution like *Messiah*, and one that is arguably still more involving, and more personal. A child performer in this work might agree with Lord Clark, who wrote: 'To sit in Orford Church, where I had spent so many hours of my childhood dutifully waiting some spark of divine fire, and then to receive it at last in the performance of *Noye's Fludde*, was an overwhelming experience.'

In 1958 Britten and Imogen Holst collaborated on a literary venture. This was a book about music for young people, *The Story of Music*. Since you cannot write about the history of music without discussing its nature, the title was later changed to *The Wonderful World of Music*. The idea seems not to have been Britten's initially ('he agreed to collaborate', says Eric Walter White), and Imogen Holst did much of the actual writing. In a letter to her from abroad he suggested a rewording of a passage that seemed to suggest a 'nature versus art' situation and offered an alternative: 'an artist ... has to create something that will have a life of its own, with the vitality of Nature's own creations'. On recent 'serial' music the two authors attempted a cautious objectivity ('Some think that it does not matter what style a composer chooses to write in, as long as he has something definite to say and says it clearly'); but in fact Britten cared little for

Schoenberg or Webern and even less for post-Webernian electronic developments, which in his view failed to communicate. A year or two later he was to speak out more frankly about such new music:

> . . . I am seriously disturbed by its limitations. I can see it taking no part in the music-lover's music-making. Its methods make writing *gratefully* for voices or instruments an impossibility, which inhibits amateurs and children. I find it worrying that our contemporary young composers are not able to write things for the young or amateurs to play and sing.

(To anticipate, it may well be partly due to Britten's quiet influence that such pieces as Peter Maxwell Davies's *Kirkwall Shopping Songs*, written for schoolchildren on Orkney in 1979, are naïvely simple in a way that would have been inconceivable from this 'advanced' composer twenty years before. Britten himself, however, is never naïve, even in his most technically simple music he is not obvious or crude.)

In the summer of 1958 Britten composed a *Nocturne* for tenor and chamber orchestra. It is a companion piece to the *Serenade* of fifteen years before, its poetic texts dealing now with night instead of evening, of similar length and also ending with a setting of a sonnet, this time Shakespeare's profound love poem 'When most I wink'. But it is a darker work; as Britten was later to say in a broadcast interview, the night 'can release many things which one thinks had better not be released', and he called his Wordsworth setting in the *Nocturne*, which describes a dream about the French Revolution, 'very nightmarish'. Nevertheless the *Nocturne* is lyrical and often sensuously beautiful. Peter Pears sang it for the first time on 16 October 1958 in Leeds. Some five weeks later he and the composer performed a shorter vocal cycle of poems by the German Hölderlin at Schloss Wolfsgarten as a fiftieth birthday present for Prince Ludwig of Hesse. 'They are short – just fragments – perhaps ten minutes in all,' Britten said in 1961, 'but I believe they are probably my best vocal works so far.'

In 1959 Britten received an honorary doctorate in music from Cambridge University. Appropriately, he was at this time involved with a commission from another university, that of Basle in Switzerland, for a cantata commemorating its six hundredth anniversary. The *Cantata Academica* totally belies its serious-sounding name; its musical 'devices' of inversion, canon, fugue and even a twelve-note (i.e. serial) theme are used very person-ally and serve only to create a feeling of delight – musical learning without a suspicion of dryness. This work for four soloists, chorus and orchestra is one of Britten's most exuberant. The Basle première was on 1 July 1960; in England the Cam-bridge University Music Society performed it and gave their Doctor of Music an ovation; and the composer also attended a student performance at the Royal Academy of Music in London. 1959 also saw the composition of a strikingly intense *Missa Brevis* for the boys of Westminster Cathedral in London and their choirmaster George Malcolm. At Aldeburgh the Jubilee Hall was enlarged and variously improved, and after the annual festival it was decided (in August) that Britten should write a new opera for the 1960 festival. He wrote some months later: 'As this was a comparatively sudden decision there was no time to get a libretto written, so we took one that was ready to hand ... I have always loved *A Midsummer Night's Dream*.' There was time for a holiday in Venice. Then he started work on the Shakespeare opera in October and finished it in April – 'seven months for everything, including the score ... the fastest of any big opera I have written,' he wrote. This was in spite of bouts of influenza: he kept on working, saying, 'I find that one's inclination, whether one wants to work or not, does not in the least affect the quality.' He and Peter Pears had worked out their own libretto, cutting out early scenes from the original play: a skilful compression that one would never suspect without knowing the play, any more than one does in the similarly cut *Otello* libretto that Boito made for Verdi.

A Midsummer Night's Dream had its first performance on 11 June 1960 in the reconstructed Jubilee Hall at Aldeburgh, as part of the Thirteenth Festival, and was an unqualified success. *The Times* critic Frank Howes, hitherto not always favourable to Britten, voiced a generally held opinion when he called the work '*tout court* a great English opera'. Of course Shakespeare's classic comedy provided a story to which none could conceivably object: doubtless after *Billy Budd* and *The Turn of the Screw* some were relieved to find some 'proper' love duets, and, as Howes noted, the 'ordinary emotions ... strongly and truly conveyed'. But there was (of course) more to the critical acclamation than relief that this time Britten had chosen to set an English classic without sinister psychological undertones: the sustained skill of the music, with its different sound-worlds for lovers, rustics and fairies, was immediately recognised. Within a year of the Aldeburgh première, the *Dream* was performed in ten opera houses outside England, including that of Tokyo. Early in 1961 it came to Covent Garden in London; a celebrated Shakespearian actor, Sir John Gielgud, produced and Georg Solti conducted. 'Ben attended many of my rehearsals in London. We had a wonderful relationship ... I adored working with him,' Solti was to write some years later.

In 1960 Britten decided to revise *Billy Budd*, compressing four acts into two and losing some music in the process although increasing dramatic tautness: the new version was broadcast by the BBC on 13 November of that year and Covent Garden was to stage it in 1964. In September 1960, attending a London performance of Shostakovich's First Cello Concerto in the company of the Russian composer, Britten met the exceptionally gifted soloist, Mstislav Rostropovich, for whom this work had been written, and agreed to write a sonata for him. He sent the score of the new sonata to the cellist in the Soviet Union in January 1961. Not long afterwards Rostropovich passed through London, and recalled their meeting in Britten's flat. Both men were apparently nervous. 'Ben said, "Well, Slava, do you think we have time for a drink first?" I said, "Yes, yes," so we both drank a large whisky. Then Ben said: "Maybe we have time for another one?" "Yes, yes," I said. Another large whisky. After four or five very large whiskies we finally sat down and played through the sonata. We played like pigs, but we were so happy.' No doubt the story is substantially true, although as Britten disliked getting tipsy the ebullient Russian cellist may have exaggerated a little. The first public performance of the sonata, by himself and the composer, was on 7 July 1961, at Aldeburgh.

In 1961 Britten composed a major sacred work, his *War Requiem*, in which the bitter anti-war poems of Wilfred Owen were placed, by a stroke of imaginative genius, alongside the timeless and universal Latin text of the Mass for the Dead. The commission had come in connection with the rebuilt Coventry Cathedral which stands now beside the ruins of the medieval building destroyed by bombing in the 1939–45 war, and Britten's idea, as a lifelong pacifist, was to make a statement about war's futility and at the same time to express his deep sympathy with man's self-inflicted suffering. He dedicated the work to four friends killed in the war and preceded his score with Owen's words, 'My subject is War, and the pity of War ... all a poet can do is to warn.' As soloists he had the idea of choosing three singers from different countries involved in the European conflict: Peter Pears from England, the soprano Galina Vishnevskaya (Rostropovich's wife) from the Soviet Union and the baritone Dietrich Fischer-Dieskau from Germany. However, this symbol of the healing of wounds was not in fact realised until the work was recorded in January 1963, because Vishnevskaya was not available for the Coventry première; on that occasion, 30 May 1962, the soprano part was sung by Heather Harper, while Meredith Davies conducted the City of Birmingham Orchestra and Britten directed the chamber ensemble that accompanies the Wilfred Owen settings. As with *A Midsummer Night's Dream*, critical opinion of the *War Requiem* was unanimous. 'A major masterpiece' was Frank Howes's simple phrase, while in the view of Percy Young the composer here achieved 'a breadth of expression that puts the work among the major achievements of religious art'. The Master of the Queen's Music, Sir Arthur Bliss, not long after this and in my hearing, described Britten as England's greatest living composer.

On 22 October 1962 Britten was made an Honorary Freeman of Aldeburgh. 'I am proud,' he said on that occasion, 'because this honour comes from people who know me ... As I understand it, this honour is not given because of a reputation; it is – dare I say it? – because you really do know me, and accept me as one of yourselves, as a useful part of the Borough; ... and this is, I think, the highest possible compliment for an artist. I believe ... that an artist *should* be part of his community, *should* work for it, with it, and be used *by* it. Over the last hundred years this has become rarer and rarer, and the artist and community have both suffered as a result.' He did not oppose new artistic ideas; nevertheless there was 'all the difference in the world between Picasso ... or Henry Moore, and the chap who slings paint on canvas; between Stravinsky and electronic experimenters.' For Britten, artistic creativity had nothing to do with anarchy, nor with flippant irresponsibility. What it *had* to do with was love, intelligence, dedication, hard work – and again, *love*, for music and the people who made it and the world in which it was made.

In 1963 Britten celebrated his fiftieth birthday. Before the birthday itself on St Cecilia's Day, he wrote two major works – a Cello Symphony for Rostropovich, and the *Cantata Misericordium* for the International Red Cross, on the Good Samaritan parable. He took part, in March, in a Festival of British Music that was mounted in the Soviet Union; in both Moscow and Leningrad there were performances of his music including the *Sinfonia da Requiem* and the orchestral Interludes and Passacaglia from *Peter Grimes*, while Peter Pears performed the *Serenade*, *Winter Words* and the *Six Hölderlin Fragments*. In a *Pravda* interview he was reported as thinking the Soviet public 'wonderful' – though presumably a contrary opinion would not have been printed. In fact both Britten and Pears liked Russia and their hosts very much. They already had a number of friends, including Shostakovich (whose music Britten had liked even before the war), the Rostropovich family and the pianist Sviatoslav Richter. In 1964 *Peter Grimes* was to be given its Soviet première. In the meantime the fiftieth birthday year was marked by various events. A book edited by Britten's friend Anthony Gishford, called *Tribute to Benjamin Britten*, was published by Faber and Faber. It contained essays and greetings from many friends: there is a touchingly warm one from Francis Poulenc, finding the composer '*glorieux comme un jeune Verdi*', and Rostropovich wrote that in time to come people would celebrate his 150th and 200th birthdays ... 'I foresee these jubilees and congratulate you in advance'. Oxford University conferred upon him an honorary degree, and Michael Tippett dedicated a Concerto for Orchestra to Britten 'with affection and admiration'. On 12 September 1963, a whole Promenade Concert at London's Albert Hall was devoted to his work, while a new *Peter Grimes* production, opening on 16 October, was directed by Basil Coleman at Sadler's Wells. On the birthday itself, 22 November, *Gloriana* was given in a Royal Festival Hall concert performance, in the presence of a happy and youthful-looking composer; sadly, that evening the American President John F. Kennedy was killed and the news darkened the final stage of the birthday celebrations.

9

With Aschenbach
in Venice (1964-76)

CHORUS

p solemn

'They en-ter in-to the house of the Lord.'_____

Death in Venice, Act I

The *War Requiem* had a world-wide success comparable to that of *Peter Grimes* nearly twenty years before. By the end of 1963 it had been given in more than a dozen foreign cities including Berlin, Paris, Prague and Boston. The composer conducted a gramophone performance for Decca in January 1963 which sold 200,000 copies within five months. Everyone seems to have agreed with Peter Pears: 'I don't think there is any doubt that it is a masterpiece.' The work even reached Leningrad, where its religious content might have been thought unacceptable.

Britten took all the tributes with a degree of satisfaction, but with equanimity also. It was much pleasanter to be praised than (as so often in the past) blamed. But he was not amenable to being 'assessed', summed up, placed in some pigeon-hole of convenient historical and aesthetic reference. Indeed he described as dangerous the kind of commentary made upon music by 'critics who are already trying to document today for tomorrow'. He said that he did not know whether he would prove to be 'a ripple or a wave' in the river of musical history. 'I do not write for posterity ... I write music, now, in Aldeburgh ... for anyone who cares to play it or listen to it.' He remarked too that under the sheer weight of fiftieth birthday tributes and celebrations he felt 'that he was really dead'. It was an uncomfortable feeling, and he overcame it in the obvious way, by getting on with his work. Whatever others might say, he felt disinclined to rest on his laurels: 'I haven't yet achieved the simplicity I should like in my music.'

Early in 1964 Britten was in the Soviet Union to conduct the first performance of his Cello Symphony, given on 12 March in the Great Hall of the Moscow Conservatory with Mstislav Rostropovich (its dedicatee) as soloist and the Moscow Philharmonic Orchestra. Some weeks later he was in Budapest, where he met two twelve-year-old musical twins, Zoltán and Gábor Jeney, one a flautist and the other a violinist, and both competent also on the piano. As he later recalled,

> ... they approached me and charmingly, if forcefully, asked me to write them a work. Though I claimed that I was too busy, my refusal was brushed aside; however, I insisted on one small bargaining point: I would do it only if they would write me a long letter telling me all about themselves, their work and their play – in *English*. I felt safe. After a week or two, however, the letter arrived in vivid and idiosyncratic English, and I felt I must honour my promise.

He was to write a 'quartet for two players' for the boys early in the following year, the 'Gemini Variations' on a theme by the Hungarian composer Kodály (between them they had to play the flute, violin and piano duet) and brought them over to give the première at the 1965 Aldeburgh Festival, while the guest of honour in the audience was the 83-year-old Kodály himself. Both boys were later to become professional musicians.

Somehow during his travels early in 1964, Britten found time to compose a new opera, or 'parable for church performance'. This was *Curlew River*, with a libretto by William Plomer based on the Japanese *Nō* drama *Sumidagawa* which he had seen eight years previously in Tokyo. Plomer had at first thought the idea impossible, but Britten was persuasive: and the composer began work in February in 'a cold Venice' (Peter Pears in a postcard to me) where the monks' robing before Mass in San Giorgio Maggiore impressed him so much that he decided to incorporate this ritual into his own work. The story of the noblewoman seeking her child and crossing the river to find his shrine and hear his spirit voice was transferred from medieval Buddhist Japan to the fenland of medieval England. When the score was finished just before Easter in Aldeburgh, it was clear that Britten had learned much from the Japanese piece: the flute writing and percussion ensemble of small drums, bells and gong were especially evocative, while the use of a tenor instead of a female singer for the mother's role was equally stylised and authentic. There was no conductor; instead different singers or instrumentalists 'led' the music in turn. For the première in Orford Church on 12 June the producer-designer Colin Graham aimed at 'control, clarity and concentration'. Britten himself had this to say: 'There is nothing specifically Japanese left ... but if stage and audience can achieve half the intensity and concentration of that original drama I shall be well satisfied.' *Curlew River* was dedicated 'in friendship and admiration' to Michael Tippett.

Mstislav Rostropovich was another dedicatee who between 1961 and 1971 was to have a Cello Sonata, the Cello Symphony and no less than three unaccompanied suites written for him. ('Rostropovich got his works by bullying me,' Britten once admitted wryly.) On 18 June 1964 Rostropovich gave the Cello Symphony its English première at the Aldeburgh Festival, and the following month he and Britten recorded the work in London together with the Haydn C major Concerto for which Britten provided cadenzas. Also in July Britten travelled to Aspen, Colorado to receive the first Aspen Award of $30,000 for service to 'the humanities'. At the ceremony on 31 July he expressed his belief in music that might 'speak to or for' people; he spoke also of the danger of pressures upon the artist, whether to write 'true proletarian music' or practise 'the latest *avant-garde* tricks', and of the economic difficulties of a musician's life. He made cautionary comments on the recording and mass communication of music: these, he thought, were no substitute for the intense experience of live music-making in which every performance is a different re-creation of an original.

It was at this time that after thirty years Britten decided to change his publisher. Since the death of Erwin Stein in 1958 he had become less satisfied with his Boosey & Hawkes relationship, and when in 1964 Faber & Faber (in the person of Donald

Mitchell) responded to his idea that they might start music publishing, he was happy to sign a new contract with them. His first piece to be published by Faber Music Ltd was the 'Nocturnal' for guitar which he had composed for Julian Bream, a sombre meditation on a Dowland song ('Come, heavy sleep') that has, in the composer's words, 'some very disturbing images': of its eight sections, Nos 2–4 are marked 'Very agitated', 'Restless' and 'Uneasy'.

1965 began with a trip to India on holiday with Peter Pears. He started work on the 'Gemini Variations' for the Hungarian twins, and he also gave thought to a new song cycle with piano which was to be performed by Dietrich Fischer-Dieskau and himself at the Aldeburgh Festival on 24 June. Peter Pears helped him select texts from Blake's poetry including 'The Chimney-Sweeper', 'The Tyger' and 'Ah, Sun-flower!' The *Songs and Proverbs of William Blake* take into account the dark timbre of Fischer-Dieskau's voice, compassionate and world-weary, which Britten already knew in his own music from the *War Requiem* and the *Cantata Misericordium*, and the use of a twelve-note series makes the work seem all the more introverted. As Peter Evans has commented, 'resignation rather than resolution seems the outcome of this cycle of Blake's Experience; it is not fortuitous that Britten's first baritone songs sound the most sombre note yet heard in his vocal music.' Eight days before the Blake songs' première, he conducted a performance of Mozart's B flat major Piano Concerto, K. 595, in Blythburgh Church with Sviatoslav Richter as soloist. The celebrated Russian pianist came in with his second entry instead of his first, as Britten remembered with sympathetic amusement ('I could see no future at all at that moment'), but fortunately then recovered neatly and the performance did not collapse. Immediately after the festival Britten set to work on a United Nations commission. *Voices for Today* was an anthem to words by diverse writers from all periods and countries (from Lao Tzu and Jesus Christ to Camus and Yevtushenko) that have in common the theme of reconciliation and love between earth's peoples; it began and ended with Christ's admonition, 'If you have ears to hear, then hear!' and the listener may be reminded of Wilfred Owen's words on the title page of the *War Requiem*, 'All a poet can do is to warn.' *Voices for Today* had simultaneous premières in New York, Paris and London on 24 October 1965, marking the twentieth anniversary of the United Nations. The UN Secretary-General, U Thant, said on that occasion: 'To Benjamin Britten, the ideal of peace is a matter of personal and abiding concern ... Today he speaks for all of us, with an eloquence we lack, in a medium of which he is a master.'

It was time for another holiday. Britten and Pears had within the last two years made three trips to the Soviet Union, the last of these being a tour with the English Opera Group late in 1964 during which they performed *The Rape of Lucretia*, *Albert Herring* and *The Turn of the Screw*. Now Britten and Pears were invited to stay in the Composers' Home for Creative Work in Dilizhan, Armenia for three weeks in August 1965. The whole thing had been organised (at least to a certain degree) by 'Slava' Rostropovich, and he and his wife Galina Vishnevskaya – Galya for short – were with Britten and Pears throughout the holiday. After the Russian cellist had played the Cello Symphony at London's Royal Festival Hall on 1 August, they all flew out to Moscow and after two nights of exciting but exhausting Rostropovich-style hospitality in a *dacha* outside the city, there was a flight to the Armenian capital, Yerevan, and eventually a four-hour drive to Dilizhan itself. The two English musicians settled into their own 'little house'.

The Armenian holiday, as described by Peter Pears in a travel diary, was enormous fun if not exactly restful. Excursions were varied and memorable.

> The view was staggering ... The air was superb; one breathed flowers and sun, and Ben and I climbed up higher still after our coffee, and somehow the whole world was explainable, so dizzy and beautiful it was ... Today we ache ... one of Ben's toes is raw and in Elastoplast, and my knee, which was not good when I left London, is now *very* not good. However, it was a heavenly day.

Mountains, flowers and birds vied for their attention with local composers, and (somewhat to Britten's horror) the holiday culminated with a Britten Festival in Yerevan, 'all in a town without charm at a probable temperature of 95 in the shade: the prospect is simply not to be dwelt on'. In the event the festival went well (though Pears was right about the heat) and Galya Vishnevskaya was able to sing two new Britten songs from a cycle of six Pushkin poems that he had set, in Russian, during the holiday. The Russians loved the songs, which they rightly took as a compliment to their country and its poetry: 'Apart from astonishment at the feel Ben shows for the language and Pushkin, not a foot wrong anywhere, their chief emotion seemed to be simply admiration for these moving, lovable songs.' A visit to Pushkin's house and museum was another highlight of the holiday and a kind of reward after the composition of the cycle. There was a visit to Shostakovich, too, near Moscow at the end of the Russian trip; he was 'all tense' to hear the new songs and also talked of his intention to visit England for the 1966 World Cup, being 'mad about football'. The whole holiday had been a success. 'Never could any two guests have been more royally treated ... we came back with much increased friendly feelings for these marvellous people.' Britten's reputation was by now fully established in the Soviet Union. *Grimes* had already been given in Leningrad and Moscow; now the Bolshoi Theatre mounted a production of the more recent opera *A Midsummer Night's Dream* which opened on 28 October 1965.

Back at Aldeburgh, Britten started work on a new 'church parable' with his librettist William Plomer. (Peter Pears calls them 'church operas'; Plomer's irreverent label was 'choperas'.) The idea of *The Burning Fiery Furnace* came from seeing a sculpture of this biblical scene in Chartres Cathedral: the story of the three young Jews and their steadfast faith, tested in King Nebuchadnezzar's fire, was altogether more colourful than that of *Curlew River*, and Britten chose a small instrumental ensemble different from that of the earlier work and including an alto trombone and Babylonian drum. Work on the opera had to be interrupted, though, when the composer underwent an operation for his recurrent stomach trouble, diverticulitis. But *The Burning Fiery Furnace* was finished in April 1966 and received its first performance during the Aldeburgh Festival on 9 June. Two months later he finished another dramatic work, a miniature 'opera' lasting seventeen minutes that the Vienna Boys' Choir had requested a couple of years before. *The Golden Vanity* had a libretto by Colin Graham based on a ballad telling of a captain 'who lets his cabin boy drown rather than reward him with his daughter's hand for sinking the Turkish pirate ship'. Britten called it a vaudeville; the Vienna Boys' Choir were pleased that their request not to be given girls' roles had been complied with, and they gave the first performance (and an immediate complete encore) at the Aldeburgh Festival on 3 June 1967. In fact *The Golden Vanity* is a little like a miniature *Billy Budd* – the parallels are obvious – though the tone is far lighter. Another operatic project with Colin Graham as the librettist, an *Anna Karenina* for the Bolshoi Company in Moscow, was considered also at the time. But the work never materialised, for a variety of reasons: Britten's health was still delicate, the libretto itself proved difficult to shape and finally, after the Russian invasion of Prague in August 1968, the Foreign Office suggested that the commission would be out of place. What disappointment Colin Graham was to experience over *Anna*, he must have felt satisfied with his successful revival of *Gloriana* that opened on 26 August 1966 at Sadler's Wells.

1967 was one of Britten's busiest years. He preceded it with a Moscow Christmas with all his Russian friends: needless to say there was lavish hospitality from the Rostropoviches, Shostakoviches and Richters. He and Peter Pears missed seeing *A Midsummer Night's Dream*, but Sviatoslav Richter described the production as 'grandiose kitsch'. They went to Leningrad too, where in the Hermitage gallery they saw the Rembrandt *Prodigal Son* whose story was to be told in the third and last of Britten's church parables, a 'triumph of forgiveness' in which there is rejoicing over the repentant sinner. But it was concert giving and concert administration that took most of his time after he returned to England. Above all, there was a new concert hall for the Aldeburgh Festival, The Maltings at Snape, not far from his former Suffolk home, the Old Mill. The Maltings represented a vast conversion from a building designed for a purpose remote indeed from music, and the expenditure of a great sum of money also (£175,000); but the new concert hall, planned in 1965, was finished in June 1967, in time for the festival. HM the Queen opened the hall on 2 June, and Britten conducted a new overture with chorus, *The Building of the House*, with a Psalm text, describing it as true occasional music 'inspired by the excitement and the haste!' He was filmed rehearsing this new piece for a television documentary about his work made by Tony Palmer in which, for once, he was persuaded to discuss his composing methods and daily routine, and to be filmed walking his dachshund along Aldeburgh beach.

This 1967 Festival was particularly successful: the new concert hall five miles inland meant that ticket sales more than doubled over the previous year's (£44,000 compared with £20,700). After it was over, Britten settled down once again to composition, completing a Second Cello Suite for Rostropovich in August. Then in September he and Peter Pears were once again away, accompanying the England Opera Group to Montreal's Expo '67 and then going to New York for recitals followed by a British Council tour covering several of the Latin American countries.

Early in 1968 Britten started work on *The Prodigal Son*, and he began composition in Venice, just as he had done in the case of *Curlew River*: 'I adore Venice,' he used to say, calling it 'unique'. But there were negative reasons too for his choosing once again to work away from The Red House. The United States Air Force, which had a base at the nearby airfield of Bentwaters, used his house (according to Colin Graham) as a landmark for lining up their trainee jet pilots on landing approaches, and the recurrent noise upset him; Venice, by contrast, was blessedly peaceful. Also the administrative responsibilities of Aldeburgh, with its festival and buildings and planning (which seemed at times endless), had begun to weigh him down. Imogen Holst, a fellow festival director, has written of 'the strain of his very full working life' at this time: 'He had reached the stage of self-criticism as a composer when each new work was proving increasingly difficult to write . . . he wanted "to think more and more about less and less".' And perhaps to travel less. In a letter to her he wrote: 'Just off to Germany – what a life! – how I wish one could sit quietly and just get on with work; but it won't last for ever, and one day I'll be able to relax a bit, and try and become a good composer.' Occasionally he jibbed at the demands of concert-giving. But it was not only for Peter Pears's sake that it continued unabated: he himself, in other moods, repeatedly stressed that a composer should not shut himself away in a studio.

Returning from Venice, in early March 1968 Britten fell ill with fever. Nevertheless *The Prodigal Son* was finished on 22 April and Britten supervised the preparations for its première on 10 June 1968 in Orford Church as part of the Aldeburgh Festival. He dedicated it to Shostakovich, a friendly gesture that perhaps also marked the inspiration of Rembrandt's picture on this subject that he had seen in Shostakovich's native Leningrad. Later that year he took up another 'wanderer' theme: *Children's Crusade* is a setting of what he called Brecht's 'heart-rending ballad' describing the wanderings of a group of lost children through the winter landscape of war-torn Poland, into which they disappear without trace. The music, for boys' voices with keyboards and percussion, is both stark and rhythmically free: Britten told me that for this reason he had had difficulty in notating it. *Children's Crusade* was composed for the fiftieth anniversary of the Save the Children Fund and most effectively performed on 19 May 1969 in St Paul's Cathedral, London, by the Wandsworth School Choir and Orchestra under their director, Russell Burgess.

Important productions of Britten's music continued. During August and September 1968 the Edinburgh Festival built its programmes especially around Britten and a composer he loved, Schubert. (He once admitted in a radio interview that he had dreamed about meeting Schubert in Vienna and that this had 'blessed the following days in a way that I have seldom remembered in my life before'.) It was there also that he heard of the Russian invasion of Prague on 21 August: Slava and Galya Rostropovich, present with Pears and Britten in Scotland, were (according to Colin Graham) 'devastated'. He was a quiet, unfussy presence at the rehearsals under Alexander Gibson for a Scottish Opera production of *Peter Grimes*. The *War Requiem* was given at Edinburgh's Usher Hall on 1 September; Carlo Maria Giulini and Britten respectively conducted the large and the chamber orchestra. In the winter of 1968–69 preparations were made for a television recording of *Peter Grimes* in The Maltings at Snape. Britten had refused to conduct it in the technically limiting conditions of a London studio (split studios, singers watching the conductor on a screen only, and the like); so the BBC Head of Television Music, John Culshaw, brought his entire team down to Suffolk. The recording, in colour, was made in February 1969. Peter Pears sang the role he had created twenty-four years earlier, for one of Culshaw's aims was, as he said, to record 'a contemporary masterpiece with the original singer ... and with the composer as conductor' – while Britten worked from a music desk with a seven-pound jar of peppermints and a police loudhailer to preserve his voice.

The television *Peter Grimes* was shown on BBC-2 on 2 November 1969. But in the meantime, tragedy had struck the Aldeburgh Festival when the new concert hall at Snape, The Maltings burned down during the night of 7–8 June, following the opening day of the festival. Perhaps a careless cigarette end was responsible; at any rate, the cause was never established. Astonishingly, the festival went on as planned: even the stage production of Mozart's *Idomeneo* was successfully transferred to Blythburgh Church. Britten, who might have despaired, instead felt a 'wild, hysterical courage', and as soon as the festival ended the work of rebuilding began. There was, of course, the insurance money, and Britten and Pears gave recitals in aid of the reconstruction in both New York and Boston during October. The work went quickly ahead, and the new hall, with 'expensive sprinklers whose efficiency we hope we shall never have to put to the test, but which are not designed to cool off musical enthusiasm' and several other improvements not concerned with safety matters, was ready to receive HM the Queen on 5 June 1970 in time for the festival. The cost now was £225,000.

During 1969 Britten had composed comparatively little. His new music of this year included a Harp Suite for the Welsh harpist Osian Ellis and a song cycle for Peter Pears, *Who are these children?*, to poems by the Scotsman William Soutar (1898–1943) of a dark intense sadness ('The blood of children stares from the broken stone'). He also continued a practice of revising and reviving youthful pieces hitherto unpublished, of which there had been four since 1966, with a set of Five 'Walztes' (in 1925, spelling was not his strongest point) for piano.

Three Britten operas – *Peter Grimes*, *The Burning Fiery Furnace* and *Billy Budd* – had received television performances and proved more than *succès d'estime*. Now Britten set to work on a full-scale commission, which he had accepted in 1967 for a new opera conceived especially for the television screen. *Owen Wingrave* was a subject Britten had been thinking about for several years: this story by Henry James tells of a young man of military family whose heroic pacifism in the face of pressures from both family and fiancée ends with his death in a haunted room. Britten himself (as an unpopular wartime pacifist) could strongly identify with Owen, whose pacifist *credo* in Act II is an affirmation of his own belief – 'Peace is not silent, it is the voice of love.' As he had done for his earlier Henry James opera, *The Turn of the Screw*, he chose Myfanwy Piper as librettist, and after some months of discussions he composed the music in the spring and summer of 1970, fitting the work around a concert tour of Australia and New Zealand. The television recording of *Wingrave* took place at The Maltings in the bitterly cold weather of November 1970 and the opera was screened on 16 May 1971. It had been sold in advance to some seventeen international television companies: in Colin Graham's words, it thus provided 'a wonderful opportunity for Britten to make his personal statement about war and the empty glory of heroism, in the context of the Vietnam war and the shooting of the students demonstrating against it on Kent campus'.

Though *Owen Wingrave* was a success, it was not a triumph. A sympathetic critic, Andrew Porter, wrote that its 'musical manners and gestures, timbres, and tricks of utterance were commonly judged masterly but somewhat disappointingly familiar'. Britten himself was never at ease with the role of Owen's fiancée Kate (Mrs Piper says he thought her 'an impossible and arrogant girl') and Janet Baker, who played the role, 'could never get over her dislike of the unfortunate girl' – while at thirty-seven she was also too old for the part. Colin Graham was co-director with a BBC producer, but felt he was 'there very much on sufferance, at Britten's request, and . . . had little or no influence on the artistic conception . . . the final effect of the opera on the screen lacked impact'. Britten was ill during much of the filming, and 'was inevitably presented with *faits accomplis* very often not to his liking'. Indeed one suspects a lack of clear focus, unusual indeed where Britten was concerned. As Graham puts it: 'Although the opera was conceived for television, Britten constantly had the theatre in mind for the work's final homecoming. While he was composing, he said he feared *Owen* would finally be completely successful only on the stage' – though Peter Pears now thinks it did work best on television. *Owen Wingrave* did reach the stage, in fact, on 10 May 1973 at Covent Garden. But Britten himself was unable to conduct the performance (it was directed by Steuart Bedford); two days previously he had undergone major heart surgery in London.

The heart operation was still three years away when Britten composed *Owen Wingrave* in 1970. But from this time onwards his recurrent illness, of various kinds including a general lassitude, increasingly handicapped and depressed him. It was oddly coincidental that at the 1970 and 1971 Aldeburgh Festivals respectively he conducted two works preoccupied with death, Shostakovich's Fourteenth Symphony (which was actually dedicated to him) and Mozart's *Requiem*. After the latter performance ended, as Imogen Holst has written, people 'were distressed to see how white and drawn he looked'; he had to apologise for being so carried away emotionally. He seemed now to need a refuge even away from Aldeburgh and bought, in 1970, a cottage, Chapel House, at Horham, a village in the depths of the Suffolk countryside, some twenty miles north-west of Aldeburgh; this became a retreat whose address was a closely guarded secret. Even so he did not cut himself off entirely. In April 1971 he participated in a British Music Week in Moscow and Leningrad, and had with him the score of a new Cello Suite (No. 3!) for Rostropovich, which quotes the Russian *Kontakion*, the Hymn for the Departed. Back in England on 9 June, he conducted Elgar's *Dream of Gerontius*, with Peter Pears as the tenor soloist, at The Maltings as part of the Aldeburgh Festival. Between September 1970 and September 1972 he conducted several Maltings recordings: Purcell's *Fairy Queen* in a realisation by himself and Imogen Holst, *Owen Wingrave*, his own Piano Concerto with Sviatoslav Richter as soloist (who learned it 'entirely off his own bat', Britten told me), Bach's *St John Passion*, *The Dream of Gerontius*, and Schubert's 'Unfinished' Symphony. And he still managed to make time for an ever-increasing correspondence with those young musicians – probably a hundred or more – who wrote to ask for advice and encouragement or simply to express their liking for his music. To one young schoolboy, Richard Pantcheff, he wrote a characteristic postcard: 'Thank you for writing me such a nice letter. I am glad you sing so much of my music, & like it. I hope that *Noye's Fludde* goes well. Are you in it? With love, Benjamin Britten.' Another postcard exhorted this young musician: 'Go on writing won't you – but you *must* have some tuition in composition, helping you to write down your ideas (some of them *good* ones) & to arrange them properly for orchestra. Also, look how other composers do it (write for instruments etc) – Love, B.B.'

It was in November 1970 that Britten asked Myfanwy Piper if she would once again work with him on a new opera. The story was to be Thomas Mann's novella *Death in Venice*: it was one he had had in his mind for some years. 'My first thought when I heard its subject was that it was impossible,' she recalls. 'The second that if Britten said so, it could be done.' The story is a celebrated one, of a middle-aged writer called Aschenbach, eminent but alone, who on holiday in plague-stricken Venice falls in love with a young Polish boy, Tadzio; he sees in him the embodiment of 'real' (as opposed to artistically-created) beauty, but can never quite bring himself to speak to the boy. Finally he dies strangely fulfilled. Did Britten himself sometimes feel, as one of Mann's characters did (in another work, *Tonio Kröger*), 'sick to death of having to represent what is human without having myself a share in it'? Did he feel, as Nietzsche had done, that an artist was 'forever shut off from reality' yet yearned 'to venture into the most forbidden territory'?

Death in Venice was, of course, written for Peter Pears, for whom Aschenbach was an ideal role. Is Colin Graham (the first stage producer of *Death in Venice*) justified in suggesting that 'of all his works, this one went deepest into Britten's own soul'? It does seem to be the most personal of his operas, in that he could identify with the person of Aschenbach, the artist whose self-discipline is undermined by hopeless love, 'so onesided an affair ... absurd'. In his declining health, he understood only too well Aschenbach's threatened mental and physical stability in the feverish heat of a sick Venice, a city which he adored (his own word) and in which he too had holidayed and worked. He knew that Thomas Mann had in Venice actually experienced the events of the story before writing his novella, admitting homosexual desire to be 'a way of feeling that he honoured'. Luchino Visconti's film of *Death in Venice*, made in 1970 but not seen by Britten, actually made Aschenbach a composer, whom the Italian director, with some justification from Mann, modelled on Mahler; Mahler had died in 1911, the year of the novella, of heart disease, and while writing his opera (with Mahler's picture on his studio wall) Britten was told a heart operation was essential if he was to live. Furthermore, *Death in Venice*, though in part a homosexual love story, was emphatically not (as Dirk Bogarde, the film Aschenbach, has pointed out) an account of a 'dirty old man' chasing a young boy: it was a parable that questioned the nature of art, of beauty, love, wisdom and innocence. As Peter Pears has said, 'Aschenbach asks ... what it is he has spent his life searching for. Knowledge? A lost innocence? And must the pursuit of beauty, of love, lead only to chaos? All questions Ben constantly asked himself.' Britten himself said only: 'I wanted passionately to finish this piece before anything happened.'

Britten went to Venice in October 1971 in the company of Myfanwy Piper and her husband John, who was to design the new opera. There they could absorb atmosphere, for the city had changed far less than most in the sixty years since the original story; they could listen to and later utilise the traditional gondoliers' cries that serve as street signals in the network of canals. Britten heard the city's bells, whose sounds were also to feature in the opera, and kept an ear open for popular airs and vocal timbres: in the end, with a little native help, the collaborators were able to use some genuine Venetian dialect. Some of the opera was written at Schloss Wolfsgarten, where the composer stayed in the spring of 1972 with his friend Peg Hesse (Prince Ludwig had died in 1968); but the bulk of the work was done in the peace of Horham. He had there an extraordinarily calm view over fields, offering space and silence. ('Night and silence – these are two of the things I cherish most,' he once said.) On his studio walls there were pictures of Frank

Bridge, Erwin Stein and the tragic daguerreotype of Chopin made in the year of that composer's death, also portraits of Mozart and Mahler: these dead figures were to become close and-friendly spiritual companions.

It was in 1972, when Britten was writing *Death in Venice*, that his doctors told him that he had a faulty heart valve, and that without an operation to replace it he could not expect to live much longer than two years. The news was perhaps half-expected: 'I was quite ready for that,' he said, 'because I felt very bad.' The second act of the new opera was written at a feverish pace, not unlike the *Donne Sonnets* long before, when he had also written of death under the influence of illness. 'I was rather difficult to cope with ... But work is a funny thing, and while I was still busy on the opera I had good days and forgot about my condition. But I did feel rotten, and unable to go upstairs without stopping on the way. And there is no doubt that working on such a huge score as *Death in Venice* was extremely exhausting.' He still found time to thank his schoolboy correspondent Richard Pantcheff for his letters, writing on 29 January 1973 that 'I enjoy getting them, altho' I can't always answer – how would you like to have to write nearly 700 pages of Full Score by the Spring!' He had finished his sketch of the opera on 17 December 1972; the score was completed the following March, in which month he and Pears were also able to visit Peg Hesse at Wolfs-garten for her birthday on 18 March.

Britten's operation took place on 8 May 1973 at the National Heart Hospital in London. It was only partially successful, though: the heart valve was replaced, but during surgery he also suffered a slight stroke that left him without the full use of his right arm and generally weakened. It was clear almost at once that his career as a performing pianist and conductor was over. As his doctor, Ian Tait, put it, he 'had to come to terms with the fact that he was not going to get better in the way he had hoped ... he did get depressed, and felt that everything he cared for most had been taken from him.' This was a very bad time indeed. Nevertheless the 'pins and needles' feeling on his right side improved steadily. 'I've been very ill & writing still is v. difficult,' he admitted in a postcard to Richard Pantcheff; but he could at least use his hand to write. Much of 1973 was spent recuperating at Horham, finding reassurance in reading Haydn and Eliot. He had to miss the *Death in Venice* rehearsals and even the première (conducted by Steuart Bedford on 16 June at The Maltings). But he could derive some satisfaction from the generally favourable response from press and public: 'one can only marvel at the score', wrote the *Sunday Times* critic, Felix Aprahamian, while Winton Dean in the *Musical Times* saluted Pears's Aschenbach as 'one of his greatest performances'. Little by little the composer felt himself to be getting better. On 12 September he attended a semi-private performance of *Death in Venice* at The Maltings, and the Covent Garden audience were delighted to applaud him when he saw the opera there on 18 October. He was able to take a motoring trip to Wales with Pears and to stay at Barcombe, Sussex, with his friends Donald and Kathleen Mitchell. But he was unable to take part in the events marking his sixtieth birthday, which included an all-Britten day on BBC Radio 3 and an Albert Hall concert.

About a year after his operation, Britten started composing again. At first, even when physically able once again to write, he had felt unable to work at music: 'I had no confidence in my powers of selection. I was worried too about my ideas.' But as he told Alan Blyth in December 1974: 'I suddenly got my confidence back about five months ago, and now composing has become, apart from anything else, a marvellous therapy. Now that I can write again I have the feeling of being of some use once more.' He revised an early String Quartet in D major written in 1931 and, encouraged by his publisher Donald Mitchell, reshaped his 1941 opera *Paul Bunyan* that had lain withdrawn and unperformed for over thirty years. Then in July 1974 he returned to real composition with a canticle to Eliot's poem *The Death of Saint Narcissus*, which he dedicated to the memory of William Plomer, who had died in 1973. Since he could no longer play for Peter Pears he composed for tenor and harp, and Peter Pears and Osian Ellis gave the first performance in January 1975.

From 1974 Britten had a constant companion in the person of his Scottish nurse Rita Thomson. Very experienced with cases of heart disease, she found him a good patient who accepted that he should follow the advice of a fellow professional, while he in turn found in her a loving yet wholly practical friend, watchful that he should not over-tire himself yet recognising his absolute need to compose, even if only for an hour or so each day. She went with him to the Mitchells in Sussex in the summer of 1974 and to Wolfsgarten in October, where he worked on a new Suite on English Folk Tunes, *A time there was ...*: its title referred back to the last of his Hardy settings in *Winter Words*. In the meantime Peter Pears had one of his greatest triumphs as Aschenbach in the New York Metropolitan Opera production of *Death in Venice*. Though unable to travel so far, the composer was at least able to talk to his friend on the transatlantic telephone.

During the following year, 1975, Britten felt a little better. He composed a set of vocal pieces, *Sacred and Profane*, for Pears and the Wilbye Consort which the singer directed. Two other vocal works were the vivid 'Birthday Hansel' of Burns settings for the Queen Mother's seventy-fifth birthday, for tenor and harp, and the dramatic cantata from Racine, *Phaedra*, for mezzo soprano and chamber orchestra. He was saddened by the death of his friend Shostakovich, from heart disease, in August. But there were happier things, such as a canal-boat holiday in May, in Oxfordshire. He went twice to Covent Garden in early July, to see *Death in Venice* and a new production of *Peter Grimes*. Then in November he made his last visit to Venice, staying at the Hotel Danieli Royal Excelsior, where a wheelchair and the care of Rita Thomson and his friends the Servaes family meant that he could visit his favourite palaces, galleries and gardens. It was in Venice on 16 November that he completed the sketch of his Third String Quartet, the last of whose five movements ('La Serenissima') makes reference to the music of *Death in Venice*.

But as 1976 began and went on into its notorious summer heat wave and drought, it became clear that the composer's health was once again failing. Nevertheless there was no question of stopping work. He rearranged his rather neglected 1950 piece, the 'Lachrymae' for viola and piano, giving it a string orchestral accompaniment, and made eight new folk song arrangements for Peter Pears and Osian Ellis. He also composed a short 'Welcome Ode' for school musicians to perform during the following year on the occasion of the Queen's jubilee visit to Suffolk. He was present at several Aldeburgh Festival performances, including the revival on 4 June of *Paul Bunyan*, a generally successful event that (in the words of *The Times* critic William Mann) 'justified the resuscitation of the work far beyond the satisfying of curiosity'; Peter Heyworth in the *Observer* found the operetta 'blessed with the lightheartedness of youth'. He also heard Janet Baker sing *Phaedra* with the English Chamber Orchestra under Steuart Bedford on 16 June; though one may regret his choice of the Robert Lowell translation rather than Racine's magnificent original French, this was still (for Peter Stadlen in the *Daily Telegraph*) 'a stunning experiment in the field of dramatic music', while another critic, Stephen Walsh, thought it 'perhaps even his most brilliant achievement since *Curlew River*'. (Though I cannot let that opinion pass unchallenged. Leaving aside the claim of such a masterpiece as *Death in Venice*, I find 'A Birthday Hansel' subtler harmonically and surer emotionally than *Phaedra*.)

Although Britten had by no means retired altogether from public life, a strict limit had now to be placed on visitors and on social events. However, there was a garden party at The Red House when it was announced on 12 June 1976 that he had been created a life peer in the Queen's Birthday Honours, as Baron Britten of Aldeburgh in the County of Suffolk. And one unexpected visitor was his friend of forty years before, Christopher Isherwood, whom he had not seen for many years. Isherwood wrote: 'I knew Ben was ill, but I didn't know how ill he was. Any emotion was bad for him···. The others left us, and Ben and I sat in a room together, not speaking, just holding hands.'

The hot summer of 1976 had taken a great deal out of the composer. As soon as the Aldeburgh Festival was over, he and Peter Pears tried to escape from the heat by going on holiday at the end of June to the Solstrand Fjord Hotel, near Bergen in Norway. True to form, he continued to work while on holiday: he started a new piece for voices and orchestra that was a setting of a poem originally dedicated to him in 1959, Edith Sitwell's 'Praise We Great Men'. But this was not to be finished. Back in Aldeburgh, he was able to hear the Amadeus Quartet rehearse his Third Quartet at the end of September. In November he was still working at the Sitwell cantata, but was physically weak and steadily becoming more so. When Slava Rostropovich called on him in late November he was 'very sick, his hands trembling', and spoke of being buried in the small churchyard at Snape. (In the event Aldeburgh was finally chosen as more suitable.)

'He used to say, what will it be like?,' his nurse Rita Thomson has said. 'And I said, well, we'll be with you and we'll just make it as gentle as possible. And he said well, is it going to be painful? And I said no, we wouldn't want it to be painful – and of course it wasn't. I said that I would be with him and probably Peter, *obviously* Peter would be with him when the time came that he was going to die.' Mentally at least, he was prepared. Peter Pears has suggested that the Folk Song Suite, *A time there was* ..., composed two years before his death, represented (say in its final slow cor anglais solo, a swan song like that of Sibelius's *Tuonela*) 'a looking back, not with regret however, but with affection for what had been, and sorrow for what now could never be. We'd faced up to what was going to come a good deal earlier than this, and he was not in any terror of dying. Not at all. I mean, I don't think he really had any particular conviction as to what was going to happen after that, but he was certainly not afraid of dying. And he died – in my arms, in fact – peacefully, as far as he could be said to be peaceful when he in fact was very ill. But there was no struggle to keep alive, except a purely physical one (which one can't help making) to breathe. But what was his greatest feeling was sadness and sorrow at the thought of leaving me, his friends, and his responsibilities. He'd always said earlier, to me, I must die first, before you, because I don't know what I would do without you.'

Britten died at 4.15 am on 4 December 1976 at The Red House. Three days later the funeral took place at Aldeburgh Parish Church. The procession passed through the town, where a muffled peal of bells was rung and flags flew at half-mast; local lifeboatmen made up a guard of honour. The Bishop of Ipswich gave a short address that ended with the words: 'Ben will like the sound of the trumpets, though he will find it difficult to believe they are sounding for him.' The choir sang the *Hymn to the Virgin* which he had composed as a sixteen-year-old boy with a lifetime of achievement before him. But now his active work was done. His closest family and friends went on to the burial in the churchyard, where the grave had been lined with rushes from the Snape marshes. The gravestone, no larger than others, reads simply: 'BENJAMIN BRITTEN 1913–1976'.

10

A time there was ... (1977–81)

Andante comodo e molto tranquillo

PETER *dolcissimo*   *senza voce*

What har — bour shel-ters peace,   a-way from

ti-dal waves, a-way from storms!

Peter Grimes, Act III

The Oxford University Diary prints in its space for 4 December 1976, the day on which Britten died, the words 'FULL TERM ends' in heavy black type. He might have appreciated the aptness of that coincidence: this composer born on St Cecilia's Day did not scorn portents. He once said that he had 'a very strong feeling that people died at the right moment'. The valedictory nature of much of his last music is clear: *Death in Venice*, *The Death of Saint Narcissus*, *A time there was ...*, *Phaedra* – the queen with poison in her veins. Martin Lovett, the Amadeus Quartet's cellist, considers that Britten regarded his Third Quartet as a swan song; and the *Sunday Telegraph* critic Bayan Northcott similarly observed that 'its passacaglia amounts in measured fugal progressions over a tolling bell motive to a final page of touchingly heaven-aspiring textures, complemented at the very end by a deep, almost Mahlerian sigh.'

Nevertheless, as is so often the case, it is misleading to paint too simple a picture. Another critic, Stephen Walsh, rightly noted that while Britten's late revisions of early compositions like the 1931 String Quartet and *Paul Bunyan* suggest 'a mind which had begun apocalyptically to take stock of its life's work', it was also true that he found revision a practical way of returning to composition after his serious illness. And although the last song in *Sacred and Profane* is called 'A Death', the medieval text is here treated with brisk and sardonic humour. Alban Berg had found in Mahler's Ninth Symphony – a work written by a man also suffering from heart disease – 'the expression of exceptional love for this earth, the longing to live at peace in it, to enjoy nature to its depths before death comes, for he comes irresistibly'. But Britten's personality was different. Less of a 'romantic' than Mahler, he faced the inevitable with a certain stoicism. His English middle-class upbringing helped restrain him from sinking into sentimentality and self-pity. He could look back over fifty years to his boyhood games of cricket and remember the lesson learned then, that everyone's innings had to come to its end; and with the recent deaths of friends like Wystan Auden, William Plomer and Dmitri Shostakovich he had learned to live with mortality. There was an emptiness, an unknown to face; but he could face it without terror. In certain moods he may have succeeded in feeling with Wilfred Owen's soldier: 'we've walked quite friendly up to Death;/Sat down and eaten with him, cool and bland', though he could not share the faith of Saint Nicolas ('Lord, I come to life, to final birth').

Warned by The Red House, the national papers had announced a few days before his death that Britten was 'gravely ill with a deteriorating heart complaint', and the obituaries were ready. Since he died on a Saturday, it was the Sunday papers that appeared first. In *The Sunday Times*, Desmond Shawe-Taylor wrote a warm tribute: 'Britten earned not only respect for a long series of fine achievements but something akin to love ... he enriched the failing store of happiness.' In the *Sunday Telegraph* Bayan Northcott recalled the uniquely atmospheric quality of the music, 'those shining, darkly bright lines and textures that could evoke a bleak sea coast or a magical nightscape so completely'. In *The Observer* Peter Heyworth noted that he 'made a larger contribution to the operatic repertory than any composer since Prokofiev, or even Strauss'.

Musicians also paid their tributes. The Master of the Queen's Music, Malcolm Williamson, said, 'Benjamin Britten preached peace through his music. We wish him the peace for which he strove in this world.' An old friend, Michael Tippett, spoke also as a fellow composer: 'Britten has been for me the most purely musical person I have ever met ... Dear, dear Ben, to the end I keep a place warm in my heart.' Yehudi Menuhin also wrote memorably:

> Thinking about him, I am most struck by his eternal youth-fulness. There was something extremely boyish about him. It accounts for his identification with young people and for how much of his work was written for children ... He would ask the public to join in his works where possible because he loved to share his enjoyment of music. He would have liked the dogs and horses, and especially the dolphins, to join in too ... If wind and water could write music, it would sound like Ben's ... He was greatly loved, like Orpheus. I shall miss him very much.

There were, of course, still those critics who even in the context of an obituary notice felt unable to join without qualification in the general praise of Britten as a great composer. Peter Heyworth's remark concerning 'his unchallenged position in the public mind as the leading British composer of his time' seems on a second reading to imply that the writer's more discriminating mind may hold another opinion. The *Daily Telegraph* critic Martin Cooper provides another case in point. On 15 June 1968 he had found 'limitations in Britten's music – the child's or adolescent's sensibility which leads him to prefer make-believe to reality, an idealised past to the uninviting present'. Now on 6 December 1976 he headed his obituary article rather curiously 'The brilliance of Britten', as if the composer were still not much more than a clever undergraduate. Once again Cooper returned to his theme of 'emotional immaturity in the man'; however, on this special occasion he went on more positively to suggest that this trait 'had its happy reflection in the artist's understanding of children and in the childlike, unspoiled capacity for wonder, for infusing new life and individuality into a familiar situation, a well-worn harmony or melodic phrase, that is a characteristic of all his best music.'

But the *Daily Telegraph*'s official, non-specialist obituary offered a tribute wholly without reserve. Headed 'Benjamin Britten, the truly towering talent of his age', it went on to declare that for the first time in three hundred years England had produced a great composer. And *The Times* for 6 December provided an obituary notice that occupied eighty column inches. Its anonymous author called Britten 'much more than the leading English composer of his time' and suggested that everything he did had had

> some relevance to his personal faith and idealism ... He was a high-minded and high-principled person ... his absolute artistic honesty was dictated by his faith, as was his contempt for power and violence. His early left-wing socialism remained with him as a moral and social, rather than dogmatically political belief ... Rarely have such artistic endowments been matched with such a sense of human responsibility for their best use.

A leading article on another page of the same *Times* issue was headed 'A Dedicated Life' and spoke of the composer giving himself equally to the practice of Christian virtues and the preaching of musical professionalism. The themes of his work were resumed:

> For the countryman nature was a constant inspiration, especially the sea; for the Christian pacifist there were sacred music, hatred of cruelty and all oppression; above all compassion for the victim and the nonconformist, and constant exploration into the world of childhood. Those themes often meet and collide in his works memorably, in *Billy Budd* and the *Children's Crusade* and *Death in Venice*.

A few days later, in the same paper, the poet Geoffrey Grigson added a personal note. Britten, he wrote, had a quality of

> kindness so unadulterated, which once experienced remained incandescent in memory. If you encountered personal kindness from this great man, you encountered what was also an element in the piercing benediction of his music. This kindness was sympathy, not condescension, a portion of that total sympathy with man and child, with existence and sentience, which made him, for instance, find the poetry he involved in his music ... I know that this Christmas many, many homes

will play the record of *A Ceremony of Carols* with a mixed
infinity of pleasure, thanks and tears.

The tributes went on for several weeks. The Performing Right
Society's journal, representing composers and publishers,
headed a short article 'Salute to a Genius' and called Britten
'an illustrious example of that still very rare phenomenon: a
creator of unmistakable, authentic genius'. In the magazine
Opera Sir George Solti used the same word, adding that 'his
departure has left an enormous emptiness'. Ernest Bradbury in
the *Yorkshire Post* wrote of 'quite obvious genius ... it seemed to
some of us, a kind of reincarnation of Mozart. He had the same
facility, the same ineffable grasp of the mysteries of music ...
For many of us, the world without Ben Britten can never again
be the same.'

Various Britten anecdotes appeared also to complement the
formal obituaries: 'human interest' stories perhaps and as such
somewhat journalistic. Yet in his case perhaps more than in that
of some other composers, stories of the man seem to illuminate
and accord with the musical personality; here too we find evidence of the instant sympathy, the practicality, the mischievous
humour. The critic Ernest Bradbury wrote of an occasion when
his two children saw Britten and Pears in the audience at a
concert in Edinburgh and asked for their autographs. 'As, oblig-
ingly as ever, they were signing, I went up behind and said:
"You probably wouldn't do that if you knew their father was a
critic." Said Ben promptly, with that marvellous screwed-up
smile: "There are critics and critics!" I can't remember what I
heard after that, but I'm sure it got a good notice.' The guitarist
Julian Bream asked Britten for a new composition, and over
lunch the composer drew a stave on the menu and wrote a chord
on it – 'Can you play that on your guitar?' Bream looked at it,
thought hard, and said 'no'. Nothing more was said until they
were leaving; then the composer picked up the menu and pushed
it into Bream's pocket. 'Try it when you get home,' he said. 'So,'
said Julian, 'I got out the old guitar, and had a go, and ... the
bastard!!' (A similar incident occurred at the first run-through of
the *Frank Bridge Variations* back in 1937, when the viola soloist
had trouble with a passage in harmonics; as Boyd Neel recalls,

Britten picked up the instrument 'and played the passage quite perfectly'.) He liked reading scores, not always by the obvious composers; Sibelius was a favourite at one time (he thought him 'neglected') but his respect for this very different master did not stop him from pointing at a passage of the Sixth Symphony and saying with a wicked humour, 'I think he must have been drunk when he wrote that!' Having described one soprano as having a face 'like the back of a cow', he added thoughtfully, 'but a *very nice* cow'.

One of the best accounts of The Red House in Aldeburgh came in a February 1977 *Gramophone* tribute by the late John Culshaw, the record and television producer who worked with Britten on many occasions, including the *War Requiem* recording and the television *Peter Grimes* and *Owen Wingrave*.

The Red House really was peace: a large, rambling place secluded from the town, to which various extensions and conversions had been added over the years. To be a weekend guest there was to relax completely; although, before his illness, Ben's own ideas about relaxation might not totally coincide with those of a city-dweller. Of course nothing was obligatory, and I enjoyed the long country walks, not least because he was an expert ornithologist, whereas I cannot tell a curlew from a duck; but I confess that more often than not I dodged the early morning swim before breakfast because, as a city-dweller, I had been awakened hours earlier by the dawn chorus of birds which those who live regularly in the country never seem to hear. By the time the birds had shut up I would be fast asleep again, and Ben and Peter would be in the pool or walking the dogs in the garden or at breakfast. One of the cruellest ironies of Ben's early death is that he had kept himself so fit. He was no kind of health fanatic, but until the final illness he enjoyed the outdoor life: he walked regularly, he swam, he played tennis. He did not smoke, but he enjoyed a drink if there was conversation to go with it. He loved good food, and the best food of all was at The Red House because it was fresh, like fish straight out of the sea with vegetables from the garden. The last time we had a meal together at The Red House, which was when there seemed to be at least a chance that his condition might not get any worse, we had grilled sprats which, he remarked, 'really are worth the awful smell they make in the kitchen'. Maybe it seems trivial to mention such things, but I don't think so, because they show the other side of a shy public figure. However well-read, however sensitive, however concerned about the state of music and indeed the state of man, he was at heart, like Elgar with whose music he eventually came to terms, a countryman. A deceptive simplicity, an earthiness, lies behind all his music, just as it lies behind the music of his beloved Schubert.

On 10 March 1977 there was a service of thanksgiving held at midday in Westminster Abbey. The Queen Mother was present, together with many other public figures, but most of the people in the packed congregation were there simply because they loved Britten's music. The Dean of Westminster spoke of 'the concern and eagerness with which he entered into life's joys and sorrows, and out of which his music was begotten and born.' He went on: 'We remember him as a composer, who by the purity of his vision and dedicated use of exceptional powers inspired both old and young to find fulfilment in making music. We think of him as the interpreter of his generation in its recoil from the horrors of war and its determination to advance a world of justice, peace and human brotherhood.' Peter Pears read the Abraham and Isaac story from Genesis 22, which had inspired Britten's second vocal canticle and recurs in the *War Requiem*; he also read from Smart's poem 'Rejoice in the Lamb'. The two hymns which the composer had included in *Saint Nicolas* were sung, and the Gabrieli String Quartet with Olga Hegedus played the slow movement of Schubert's C major Quintet. Walter Hussey, the Dean of Chichester, for whose church at Northampton *Rejoice in the Lamb* was written, gave the address. Britten was, Dr Hussey said, 'a person of deeply thoughtful moral character' rather than an orthodox churchman. He added that although he had great success, 'he was also a man who knew sorrow and disappointment ... Perhaps because of his sensitive nature he felt it especially deeply, but joy and happiness kept breaking through and finding expression in his music.

Although there was nothing whatsoever childish about him, his nature was child-like, complex and simple.'

In the 1978 New Year's Honours list, Peter Pears was knighted for his services to music. As Sir Peter Pears, he went again to Westminster Abbey on 2 November 1978 for the unveiling and dedication of a Britten memorial stone, and was accompanied at the ceremony by Sir Lennox Berkeley, another old friend who indeed had known Britten before Pears himself. A third friend, Auden (who had died in 1973) was evoked when Pears read his poem, undoubtedly meant for Britten, 'The Composer':

> All the others translate: the painter sketches
> A visible world to love or reject;
> Rummaging into his living, the poet fetches
> The images out that hurt and connect,
>
> From Life to Art by painstaking adaption,
> Relying on us to cover the rift;
> Only your notes are pure contraption,
> Only your song is an absolute gift.
>
> Pour out your presence, a delight cascading
> The falls of the knee and the weirs of the spine,
> Our climate of silence and doubt invading;
>
> You alone, alone, imaginary song,
> Are unable to say an existence is wrong,
> And pour out your forgiveness like a wine.

The memorial stone, donated by the Worshipful Company of Musicians of which Britten was an Honorary Freeman, unfortunately had the date of his death wrong by a year, a mistake that cost several hundred pounds to rectify. But embarrassment was quickly forgotten during the performance of *Saint Nicolas* that closed the ceremony: Peter Pears, the original Nicolas of 1948, was the soloist and the conductor was David Willcocks.

Another memorial to Britten was the School for Advanced Musical Studies at Snape. As early as 1953 he had said to Imogen Holst in Aldeburgh: 'we're going to have a music school here one day'. In 1973 this had begun with a weekend for singers directed by Peter Pears, and since that time it had steadily grown. In his will, published on 5 September 1977, the composer left £100,000 to establish a charitable fund that might help the school, together with the Aldeburgh Festival and the Britten-Pears Library at The Red House in which his manuscripts should remain. Some scores now belong to the nation (as the British Library) in settlement of capital transfer tax, but remain on permanent loan in the library at Aldeburgh.

As December 1976 receded, it became clear that the interest in Britten's music, and in him also as a personality, remained unusually lively. The 1977 Edinburgh Festival opened with a concert designed as a tribute to him and including his music and Walton's *Improvisations on an Impromptu of Benjamin Britten*; an Albert Hall Promenade Concert on 7 September 1977 was similarly dedicated to him and consisted of works by him and by Schubert, his old friend Sir Clifford Curzon playing the 'Trout' Quintet with members of the Amadeus Quartet and the bass player Georg Horthagel. Several new Britten recordings appeared: the revised 1931 String Quartet, *Phaedra*, *A time there was* ... under Leonard Bernstein, *Peter Grimes* with Jon Vickers in the title role and Colin Davis conducting, and the *Spring Symphony* under André Previn. Early in 1980 EMI issued a two-disc set called *Peter Pears, Benjamin Britten: The Early Recordings* that contained, among other things, the 1940s recordings of the *Michelangelo* and *Donne Sonnets*. April 1980 saw three important hour-long radio documentary programmes, containing much hitherto unpublished material from Britten's diaries and letters: they were written by the composer's literary executor Donald Mitchell and titled 'Britten: The Early Years'. The subject of the composer's homosexuality had been publicly aired as early as December 1977, when Philip Brett suggested in *The Musical Times* that *Peter Grimes* was an allegory of the homosexual condition, representing for its young composer 'the ultimate fantasy of persecution and suicide'. The matter was further discussed by Donald Mitchell and Hans Keller in a BBC radio talk, 'Britten in retrospect'; but these two men, lifelong devotees of Britten's music since (and indeed before) they had edited the valuable *Commentary on his work from a group of specialists* in 1952, cordially disagreed over the importance of this question for an understanding of the music, Keller thinking it more important than Mitchell. A later radio documentary, less sympathetic to Britten, was broadcast on 4 June 1980: its compiler, Paul Griffiths, belaboured the homosexual question in a way that embarrassed Donald Mitchell, who took part, and upset Britten's sister Beth Welford. By contrast, there was Tony Palmer's two-hour television documentary on the composer, *A time there was . . .*, a film biography for London Weekend Television broadcast on 6 April 1980, Easter Sunday. (Later in the year it was awarded the Italia Prize.) For Peter Stadlen, writing in the *Daily Telegraph*, this was 'a magnificent profile of the composer, not to be missed'. Tony Palmer had had Donald Mitchell's collaboration, and accuracy and perspective were thus assured; above all he had the full participation of Sir Peter Pears, who did not shirk the issue of homosexuality. As the television critic Sean Day-Lewis wrote, here were Britten's

> familiar adult features, ascetic and mourning lost innocence . . . from the moment when we were reminded of that marvellous transfixing moment when Pears sings of the Great Bear in *Peter Grimes* to the final memories of the life-saving nurse Rita Thomson, who made Britten's last compositions possible, tears were never far from my eyes.

On 5 August 1980 I drove from Oxford to Aldeburgh, where I had an appointment with Sir Peter Pears: before starting to write this book I had met him to go over various biographical points, and now, near the end of writing, I wanted to check some further things. An unexpected bonus was an hour's attendance at a seminar of the Britten-Pears School at Snape, Britten's most vital memorial, where a teacher was coaching young singers in Schubert while Sir Peter sat and observed the good work done. Even more satisfyingly unexpected was a meeting with Rostropovich who talked of his love not just for Britten the musician but for the man – 'so much *heart*' (the Russian word *syerdtsye*) and 'such *Russianness*'.

And so, it might seem, the tale has now been told. Yet as one obituarist wrote, we need not only write of Britten in the past tense when he is 'now all future'. The composer's foundation of an opera company, a festival with its own concert hall and a school of music reminds us of his own strong feeling for historical continuity. Four years after his death, it seems possible to stand back and consider his contribution to music. He was not a radical innovator like Schoenberg, nor even perhaps so obviously original a figure as Monteverdi or Debussy. (But then, nor do Bach and Mozart belong to the category of conscious musical explorers.) Britten's innovations were like those of Sibelius, quietly purposeful rather than striking. Nevertheless he made them. He established an operatic form, even as early as *Peter Grimes*, that was neither the separate-numbers classical technique nor the through-composed Wagnerian method; his treatment of strophic form in song was equally personal. Nonmeasured, even aleatory passages occur as early as *Albert Herring*. His chamber-orchestral writing, not only in opera but in the Sinfonietta a decade earlier, created a new sound in English music; such present-day orchestral bodies as the English Chamber Orchestra and Academy of St Martin-in-the-Fields might never have existed had it not been for his example. He extended the resources of instruments (harp, guitar, cello and not least percussion, where he even 'created' sonorities – the slung mugs of *Noye's Fludde* and the Rolls Royce spring that was the anvil in *The Burning Fiery Furnace*), and arguably too of the voice with such writing as the scherzo 'Hymn' in the *Serenade*. He left a whole new repertory of instrumental and vocal children's music from *Friday Afternoons* in 1934 to his last work, the 'Welcome Ode' of 1976; the large numbers of school pieces written today by younger composers seem inconceivable without his example, as does such a work as the Webber-Rice *Joseph and the Amazing Technicolor Dreamcoat*. (And perhaps this partnership's later 'adult' work too – for *Jesus Christ Superstar* and *Evita* have Brittenish protagonists, fated and perhaps flawed, yet sympathetic.)

The ability to integrate and reconcile 'opposites' is the musical side to Britten's pacifism and possibly the strongest single feature of his musical personality. He convincingly incorporated elements of many idioms, including jazz, into his pre-war music; while his eastern tour of the 1950s proved fruitful indeed in the melodic and instrumental techniques that are so important in the church operas and *Death in Venice*. The balletic element in that last opera is also, *mutatis mutandis*, oriental in its sharp stylisation. A musical language that can effortlessly integrate familiar old hymn tunes into original pieces (*Saint Nicolas*, *Noye's Fludde*, the Third Cello Suite also with its Russian *Kontakion*) is flexible indeed. The audience in the first and second of these works also becomes part of the performance and shares the delight resulting from such involvement. Not only the performer and listener, but also the past and present were for Britten one in a continuum: thus Dowland or Purcell could (as it were) become his colleagues, and his music at times collaborated creatively with theirs. Similarly, children and adults were brought together to give a unique quality of human depth to works as different as *A Midsummer Night's Dream* and the *War Requiem*.

Those who argue that Britten lacked emotional maturity can up to a point be refuted. Many pieces are clearly for adult performers and listeners, while the opera *Death in Venice* is in part about adulthood and an adult's failure to form an unforced relationship with a young person. (We remember also the governess, and for that matter the ghosts in *The Turn of the Screw*, though Miles is not as unreachable as Tadzio.) That the composer's adult personality was uneasy is readily admissible. But arguments that he had serious expressive limitations are also not wholly tenable. Joy and the affirmation of life shine out from *A Ceremony of Carols*, *The Young Person's Guide*, *Saint Nicolas*, *Spring Symphony* and *Cantata Academica*. Apart from *Albert Herring*, how many comic operas have been written in the twentieth century? And the often-overlooked love music for Sid and Nancy in *Herring* is happily and affectionately sexual in a wholly 'normal' context, just as Tarquinius's desire for Lucretia is animal enough and matched by appropriately virile musical gestures.

Though personally shy, Britten achieved in his music an outstanding degree of rapport with people – children and adults, performers and listeners. Sensitive people today are all too often alienated by new music which on the one hand seems crudely popular and on the other meaningless both emotionally and intellectually. Britten consciously wrote 'for human beings – directly and deliberately . . . to be of use to people, to please them, to "enhance their lives".' His success in reaching people of different ages, cultures, political and religious views, was unique among the composers of his generation.

How did he achieve his aim? Primarily, of course, through the nature of his music itself. But there was more than this: he used his performing skills and today's instruments of mass communication. He was a broadcaster from the mid-1930s. He wrote an opera, *Owen Wingrave*, especially for the newer medium of television and conducted this and three others among his operas for television performance. And despite the reservations about recorded music which he expressed in his Aspen Award speech – 'it is not part of true musical experience ... simply a substitute, and dangerous because deluding' – he made a fuller use than any contemporary of the commercial recording studio for performances both of his own music and that of other composers. As a pianist he recorded some forty issues over a period of thirty years, from 1942 to 1972; as a conductor there are forty-nine, even though his conducting career came mainly rather later; and there is even one recording of 1946 in which he played the viola. (It is of Purcell's *Fantasia upon one note*, his performance being of what might be called the title role.) Many of his recordings of his own music, made mainly for the Decca Record Company, are of outstanding artistic and technical quality: a short list restricted to stereo would have to include *Peter Grimes* (1958), the *War Requiem*, *Serenade* and *Young Person's Guide* (all 1963), the Sinfonia da Requiem (1964), *Curlew River* (1965), *A Midsummer Night's Dream* (1966), *Billy Budd* 1967), *Children's Crusade* (1969) and *The Rape of Lucretia* (1970). Among his recordings with Peter Pears there are the *Six Hölderlin Fragments* (1961) and *Holy Sonnets of John Donne* (1967), as well as a celebrated Schubert *Winterreise* (1963).

Traditionally time is the final arbiter of an artist's work – will it outlive the immediate generation for which it was created to achieve classic status? For Britten that judgement must, by definition, rest with another century. But even in the present, a mere four years after his death, it is significant just how much of his music has already lodged so firmly in the repertory, to be heard in the concert hall, in the theatre, in the church, in broadcasts and recordings, performed alike by amateur and professional. On this evidence alone, the music's survival seems beyond reasonable doubt. Also its outstanding technical skill is demonstrable, at least by musicians to musicians. But beyond this and in my view more importantly, there is something else: a humanity in Britten's work that endlessly shines out to enrich the lives of those who experience it as performers or as listeners. This contemporary composer is, I submit, also a major poet of the human condition.

Selected bibliography

Benjamin Britten: A Commentary on his works by a group of specialists, edited Donald Mitchell and Hans Keller (Rockliff, London 1952)

The first major critical work on the composer, taking the music up to *Billy Budd*. This symposium by a distinguished team of writers is still valuable.

Benjamin Britten: His Life and Operas, Eric Walter White (Faber & Faber in association with Boosey & Hawkes, London 1970)

Still a useful book for the discussion of the operas up to *The Prodigal Son*.

On Receiving the First Aspen Award, Benjamin Britten (Faber, London 1964)

A brief but invaluable *credo* from the composer.

The Operas of Benjamin Britten, edited David Herbert (Hamish Hamilton, London 1979)

A substantial, well-produced and expensive book, most useful for the preliminary essays, though it is convenient to have all the opera librettos in a single volume.

Benjamin Britten 1913–76: Pictures from a Life, compiled by Donald Mitchell with the assistance of John Evans (Faber, London 1978)

A pictorial treatment of the composer unlikely to be surpassed, by no means confined to photographs of Britten himself and containing much fascinating ancillary information.

The Music of Benjamin Britten, Peter Evans (Dent, London 1979)

A thorough and scholarly commentary upon the music, more suitable, however, to the needs of students than those of the general reader.

Benjamin Britten: A Complete Catalogue of his Published Works (Boosey & Hawkes and Faber Music, London 1973, plus supplement 1978)

Indispensable for chronology, details of premières and dedications.

Britten, Imogen Holst (Faber & Faber, London, 3rd edition 1980)

A very good children's book, well illustrated.

W. H. Auden: The Life of a Poet, Charles Osborne (Eyre Methuen, London 1980)

Britten and Auden in the Thirties: The Year 1936, Donald Mitchell (Faber, London 1981)

Valuable, for insight as well as information.

N.B. In due course Donald Mitchell's authorised biography of Britten will appear and will clearly claim its place in any collection of books on the composer.

Index

Abercrombie, Elizabeth 8

Aldeburgh: Festival 87 ff, 96, 97, 99, 100, 101, 106, 113, 117, 118, 119, 127, 128, 129, 131, 132, 133, 134, 137, 142, 154; Red House 103, 118, 133, 143, 144, 147, 151, 154

Alston, Audrey 18, 21

Amadeus Quartet 93, 143, 146, 154

Ansermet, Ernest 80

Aprahamian, Felix 141

Ashton, Frederick 86

Auden, W. H. 32–6, 39–43, 45, 49, 50, 52, 55–6, 70, 81, 90, 93, 104, 147, 153

Bach, J. S. 29, 64, 75, 137, 156

Baker, Janet 136, 143

Barbirolli, John 49

Bedford, Steuart 137, 143

Beethoven, Ludwig van 25, 29, 30, 75, 102

Beinum, Eduard van 97

Benjamin, Arthur 26, 33

Berg, Alban 25, 26, 147

Beriosova, Svetlana 117

Berkeley, Lennox 36, 38, 40, 41, 69, 82, 86, 100, 118, 153

Bernstein, Leonard 13, 81, 154

Bing, Rudolf 78, 80

Birtwistle, Harrison 100

Blades, James 32

Blair, David 117

Blake, William 96, 129

Bliss, Arthur 74, 123

Blyth, Alan 141

Bonavia, Ferruccio 11, 28

Boosey & Hawkes 33, 44, 47, 55, 61, 65, 97, 128

Boult, Adrian 37

Bowles, Mr and Mrs P. 53

Boys, Henry 34

Bradbury, Ernest 150

Brahms, Johannes 25, 74, 115

Brain, Dennis 67–8

Brannigan, Owen 70

Bream, Julian 116, 129, 150

Brett, Philip 154

Bridge, Frank 18, 20–6, 29, 34, 36, 40, 57, 73, 74, 139–40

Britten, Barbara (sister) 16, 93

Britten, Beth (sister) 16, 31, 32, 59, 60, 73, 95, 155

Britten, Edith (mother) 16–17, 31, 37, 46

Britten, (Edward) Benjamin: Aims as composer 90, 102, 119, 120, 123, 126, 128, 134, 149, 157, 158; Compositions: *Advance Democracy* 42, *Albert Herring* 15, 77, 83–7, 89, 97, 100, 130, 156, 157, *Alpine Suite* 113, *Antiphon* 116, *Ascent of F6, The* 39, 54, *Ash Grove, The* 74, *Ballad of Heroes* 42–3, 'Ballad of Little Musgrave and Lady Barnard' 70, *Beggar's Opera, The* 99, 101, *Billy Budd* 18, 98–9, 101, 103–5, 121, 122, 132, 136, 158, 149, 'Birthday Hansel, A' 142–3, *Boy was Born, A* 26, 30, 31, 53, 70, 90, 117, *Building of the House, The* 132–3, *Burning*

Fiery Furnace, The 131, 135, 156, 'Cabaret Songs' 54, *Canadian Carnival* 48, *Cantata Academica* 48, *Cantata Misericordium* 124, 129, *Canticles* 75, 141, 152, Cello Sonata 122, 128, Cello Suites 128, 133, 137, 157, Cello Symphony 71, 124, 127–8, 130, *Ceremony of Carols, A* 5, 58, 60, 63, 90, 150, 157, *Children's Crusade* 134, 149, *Curlew River* 115, 127–8, 131, 133, 143, 158, *Death of Saint Narcissus, The* 141, 146, *Death in Venice* 15, 36, 51, 92, 104, 138 ff, 142–3, 146, 149, 156–7, *Diversions* for Piano 49, 'Early one morning' 74, *Festival Te Deum* 76, *Five Flower Songs* 100, Five Walztes (Waltzes) 135, 'Foggy Dew' 74, *Friday Afternoons* 31, 156, 'Gemini Variations' 127, 129, *Gloriana* 88, 91, 99, 105 ff, 117, 125, 132, *Golden Vanity, The* 18, 131–2, Harp Suite 135, 'Holiday Diary' 33, 53, *Holy Sonnets of John Donne, The* 76–7, 140, 154, 158, *Hymn to St Cecilia* 5, 56, 58, 60, 63, *Hymn to the Virgin* 24, 144, 'I saw three ships' 27, *Les Illuminations* 35, 42, 48, 51, 54, 68, 115, *Lachrymae* 100, 142, *Little Sweep, The* 77, 83, 96, 113, *Midsummer Night's Dream* 99–100, 121–3, 131–2, 157, 158, *Missa Brevis* 121, *Mont Juic* 38, 53, *New Prince, New Pomp* 27, *Nocturnal after John Dowland* 129, *Nocturne* 120, *Noye's Fludde* 18, 90, 96, 118–19, 138, 156–7, *Occasional Overture* 82, *On This Island* 39, 54, *Our Hunting Fathers* 33, 36–7, 42, 57, *O,*

Waly, Waly 74, *Owen Wingrave* 136–7, 151, 158, *Pacifist March* 42, 79, *Paul Bunyan* 4, 53, 55–6, 70, 141, 143, 146, *Peter Grimes* 1–15, 18, 29, 48, 57–8, 60–1, 67, 70, 72, 75, 77, 80, 81, 86, 88, 97, 104, 124, 126, 131, 134–5, 142, 151, 154–6, 158, *Phaedra* 142–3, 146, 154, Phantasy for oboe and string quartet 27–8, 30–1, Phantasy for string quartet 27, *Piano Concerto* 41–2, 48, 54, 137, *Praise We Great Men* 143, Prelude and Fugue for String Orchestra 60, 64, Prelude and Fugue on a theme of Victoria 66, *Prince of the Pagodas, The* 113, 115–17, *Prodigal Son, The* 35, 132–4, *Quatre chansons françaises* 22, 53, *Rape of Lucretia, The* 76–81, 83–6, 104, 109, 130, 157–8, *Rejoice in the Lamb* 65–7, 70, 90, 117, 152, *Russian Funeral* 53–4, *Sacred and Profane* 142, *Saint Nicholas* 18, 83, 88–90, 96, 113, 147, 152, 153, 157, *Scherzo* 113, *Scottish Ballad* 57, *Serenade* for tenor, horn and strings 67, 70, 83, 120, 124, 156, 158, *Seven Sonnets of Michaelangelo* 51–2, 54, 62–3, 76, 115, 154, *Simple Symphony* 30, 48, *Sinfonia da Requiem* 4, 37, 48–9, 54, 65, 70, 115, 124, 158, *Sinfonietta* 24–7, 41, 53, 156, *Six Holderlin Fragments* 120, 124, 158, *Six Metamorphoses after Ovid* 100, *Soirées Musicales* 53, *Songs from the Chinese* 116, *Songs and Proverbs of William Blake, The* 129, *Spring Symphony* 96–7, 99, 154, 157, String Quartets: No. 1 49, 57, No. 2 60, 76, No. 3 141–3,

146, in D (1931) 141, 146, 154, unfinished 30, 42, Suite for violin and piano 33, 37, 42, *There's none to soothe* 74, *Three Part-Songs* 24, 28, 31, *Time There Was, A* 142, 144, 146, 154, *Turn of the Screw, The* 35, 99, 109, 11–13, 117–8, 121, 130, 136, 157, *Variations of a Theme of Frank Bridge* 39, 42, 44, 46, 53, 63, 150, Violin Concerto 34, 48, 53, 63, *Voices for Today* 129, 130, *War Requiem* 22, 49, 90, 122–3, 126, 129, 134, 151–2, 157, 158, 'Wedding Anthem, A' 100, 'Welcome Ode' 142, 156, *Who are these children?* 135, *Winter Words* 110, 124, 142, *Young Apollo* 47–8, *Young Person's Guide to the Orchestra, The* 82–3, 115, 157–8; Homosexuality 34–6, 95, 154–5; Honours 49, 94, 95, 101, 109, 117, 120, 123, 124, 128, 143; Ill-health 50, 66–7, 76, 92, 110, 114–15, 117, 121, 131, 134, 136–8, 140, 142, 147, 151; Methods 91 ff, 102; Nationalism in style 74–5; Obituaries 147 ff; Pacifism 4, 8, 12, 40, 43, 61, 72, 123, 136, 156; Religion 90, 149, 152 *and passim*

Britten, Robert (father) 16, 31, 46
Britten, Robert (brother) 16, 24, 31
Britten-Pears School of Advanced Musical Studies 153–4, 155
Brosa, Antonio 37, 48, 53
Burra, Peter 38

Cardus, Neville 86
Carey, Clive 78
Cavalcanti, Alberto 33, 34

Christie, John and Audrey 78, 80, 83, 85
Clark, Kenneth 62, 84, 119
Coldstream, William 34
Coleman, Basil 103–5, 106, 107, 110, 112, 124
Coleman, Charles 29
Collingwood, Lawrance 7, 9
Coolidge, Mrs Elizabeth 49, 57
Cooper, Martin 108, 148
Copland, Aaron 41, 54, 96
Crabbe, George 2, 3, 57, 61, 76, 87, 88, 97
Cranbrook, Countess of 87
Cranko, John 113
Cross, Joan 7, 8, 9, 11, 70, 77–8, 79, 86, 101, 107, 111
Crosse, Gordon 100
Crozier, Eric 5, 7–9, 78–89, 96, 98, 99, 118
Culshaw, John 135, 151
Curzon, Clifford 69, 154

Dali, Salvador and Gala 53
Davies, Meredith 123
Davies, Peter Maxwell 120
Davis, Colin 154
Day-Lewis, Sean 155
Dean, Winton 141
Debussy, Claude-Achille 19, 30, 64, 156
Decca Record Company 126, 158
de Rougement, Denis 53
Del Mar, Norman 68
Doone, Rupert 39
Dowland, John 129, 157
Duncan, Ronald 79, 83
Dyer, Olive 112

Elgar, Edward 38, 137, 152
Elizabeth II, Queen 106, 132, 135
Elizabeth, the Queen Mother 142, 152

Ellis, Osian 135, 141, 142
Elmhirst, Mr and Mrs L. 100
English Opera Group 34, 83–5, 86, 89, 97, 99, 101, 109, 113, 117, 118, 130, 133
Evans, Edgar 105
Evans, Edwin 28
Evans, Nancy 79, 101
Evans, Peter 129

Faber and Faber Ltd 124, 128
Faber Music Ltd 129
Ferrier, Kathleen 79, 80, 83
Fischer-Dieskau, D. 123, 129
Forster, E. M. 2, 88, 89, 97–9, 104

Gabrieli String Quartet 152
Gielgud, John 122
Giulini, Carlo Maria 134
Goddard, Scott 37, 66
Goodall, R. 9, 11, 78, 80, 84
Graham, C. 118, 128, 132–4
Grierson, John 32–4
Grigson, Geoffrey 149–50
Guthrie, Tyrone 7, 9, 78, 84

Hardy, Thomas 110, 142
Harewood, Lord and Lady 93, 100, 105, 114
Hawkes, Ralph 41, 84
Haydn, F. J. 64, 128, 141
Hegedus, Olga 152
Hesse, Prince and Princess of, 113–14, 116, 120, 139, 140
Heyworth, Peter 143, 147, 148
Holst, Gustav 20, 66, 100
Holst, Imogen 10, 13, 61, 66, 69, 81, 87, 91–2, 101, 105, 112–14, 119, 133, 137, 153
Horham 137, 139, 141
Howes, Frank 68, 74, 121, 123
Hudson, Miss E. 103
Humby, Betty 33

Hussey, Rev. W. 64 ff, 90, 93, 152

Insrtruments of the Orchestra, The 82
Ireland, John 24, 27, 105
Isherwood, Christopher 35, 39, 40, 43, 45, 143

James, Henry 109, 111, 136
Jeney, Zoltán and Gábor 127
Johnson, Graham 92

Keller, Hans 92, 154
Kodály, Zoltán 127
Koussevitzky, S. 4–5, 81, 96, 97

Lambert, Constant 43
Lyttleton, Oliver 84

Macnaghten–Lemare Concerts 27, 33
McNaught, William 42, 43
Macneice, Louis 39, 53
Mahler, G. 25, 36–7, 139–40, 146–7
Mandikian, Arda 111, 113
Mann, Thomas 53, 138, 139
Maud family 77, 82, 96, 97, 100, 110, 112, 117
Mayer family 46, 47, 49, 59, 60
Melville, Herman 98, 104
Menuhin, Yehudi 76, 77, 148
Mitchell, D. 35, 40, 57, 75, 88, 92, 117, 128–9, 141–2, 154–5, 162
Monteverdi, Claudio 100, 156
Moore, Henry 64, 65, 114, 124
Mozart, W. 6, 14, 25, 29, 65, 100, 129, 135, 137, 140, 150, 156

Neel, Boyd 39, 48, 63, 68, 150
Neville-Smith, Esther 88, 112
Newman, Ernest 12
Northcott, Bayan 146, 147

Ormandy, Eugene 49
Osborne, Charles 71, 90
Owen, Wilfred 122–3, 129, 147

Palmer, Tony 133, 155
Pantcheff, Richard 138, 140
Pears, Peter: Britten, partnership with 30, 35, 39, 60, 62, 67, 73, 75–6, 83, 89, 121, 135; knighthood 153; operatic roles 7, 11, 79, 86, 138, 141, 142; solo singer 40, 61, 120, 123, 124, 135, 141 *and passim*
Piper, John 79, 83–5, 104–6, 110, 139
Piper, Myfanwy 109–11, 136, 138–9
Plomer, William 50, 88, 98, 105–8, 112, 115, 127, 131, 141, 147
Potter, Peter and Mary 113, 118
Poulenc, Francis 69, 116, 124
Pritchard, John 105, 107
Prokofiev, Sergey 49, 53, 147
Purcell, H. 25, 64, 66, 73, 75, 76, 82, 84, 100–1, 137, 157, 158
Pushkin, A. S. 131

Ravel, Maurice 19, 20, 49
Reeve, Basil 34
Richter, Sviatoslav 42, 124, 129, 132, 137
Rimbaud, Arthur 35, 60
Robertson, Ethel and Rae 1–2, 57
Rostropovich, M. 122–4, 127–8, 130, 132, 134, 137, 144, 155

Sackville-West, E. 68, 70, 72, 77, 80
Sadler's Wells Opera and Ballet 1, 6, 7, 70, 78, 108, 113, 117, 124–5
Schoenberg, A. 25, 26, 29, 64, 119, 156
Schubert, F. 25, 73, 74, 93, 134, 137, 152, 155, 158

Shakespeare, W. 19, 79, 120, 121
Sharp, Geoffrey 12, 13
Shawe-Taylor, Desmond 147
Shostakovich, D. 53, 122, 124, 131–2, 134, 137, 142, 147
Sibelius, Jean 64, 144, 151, 156
Slater, Montagu 5, 6, 41
Smart, Christopher 65, 66, 152
Snape: Old Mill 39, 40–41, 60–61, 73, 132; The Maltings 132, 134–6, 141
Solti, Georg 122, 150
Stadlen, Peter 63, 143, 155
Stein, E. 61, 100, 106, 116, 128, 140
Story of Music, The 119
Strachey, Lytton 105, 106
Strauss, Richard 92, 147
Stravinsky, I. 22, 25, 80, 94–5, 100, 124
Sutherland, Graham 64, 65

Tchaikovsky, Pyotr Ilyich 29, 116
Thomson, Rita 141, 142, 144, 155
Tippett, M. 9, 69, 124, 128, 147

Verdi, G. 6, 41, 65, 67, 108, 121, 124
Verlaine, Paul 19, 22, 35
Visconti, Luchino 139
Vishnevskaya, G. 123, 130, 131

Wagner, Richard 6, 14, 99
Walsh, Stephen 143, 146
Walton, William 28, 38, 64, 72, 74, 100, 154
Webern, Anton von 25, 26, 119
White, Eric Walter 1, 90, 91, 119
Williams, Ralph Vaughan 24, 25, 38, 72, 74, 75, 108
Williams, Stephen 12, 86
Williamson, Malcolm 100, 147
Wright, Basil 33, 34, 35
Wyss, Sophie 37, 39, 48

Young, Percy 70, 123